M000117333

MY AMALFI COAST

AMANDA TABBERER

WITH PHOTOGRAPHY BY CARLA COULSON

LANTERN
an imprint of
PENGUIN BOOKS

To my beautiful son, Marco Bella,
and our Amalfi Coast.

CONTENTS

COMING HOME...

It is the end of September and the end of summer in Europe, yet the sky is as blue as the Mediterranean Sea that beckons me back to Positano on the Amalfi Coast. Until a few years ago, this had been my home for eighteen years and was where my son Marco was raised. This is our first trip back since moving to Australia – Marco, as a *Positanese*, returning to visit his dad, and me as a *forestiero* (foreigner), to see my dearest friends and to rediscover the Amalfi Coast that I have missed so much.

Marco's dad, Sergio, was the most handsome man on the Amalfi Coast. When I tell people the story of how I came to Italy to work in the fashion business, and then met and fell in love with Sergio whilst on holiday in Positano, they look at me in awe as the fairytale unfolds.

But now, on my first evening back in Positano after a year's absence, from the balcony of my apartment I look straight across town to the tiny lights of the famous five-star hotel Le Sirenuse, and remember the very first time I came here. It was August 1984, and I was living and working in Milan. I arrived in Positano on a fast hydrofoil from the island of Capri just forty minutes away, with my mum, Maggie, and two close friends. The breathtaking beauty of arriving by sea was masked only by the torrential rain falling that day. We stayed at Le Sirenuse, and spent the entire afternoon on our balcony watching the locals bail out their homes, shops, boats, bars and restaurants after the downpour. The whole town was awash, sending tourists into a frenzy, while the locals simply mopped up the mess.

Positano became not only my favourite holiday destination but also, it seemed, my destiny. My second trip here was only four weeks later. I had just started working for the new Italian fashion magazine *Lei*, and my first assignment was to go south to cover a huge outdoor fashion show put together by the renowned Italian director Franco Zeffirelli. Zeffirelli spent part of each year in Positano, where he owned one of the most beautiful villas in town, and his show was to be presented right on the main beach. So there I was, back in Positano, with pen and

ABOVE: My best friend Stefano and I,
on holiday in Positano

BELOW: The original Da Adolfo boat, which
over the years has ferried many happy diners
from Positano to Laurito beach

paper in hand, desperately trying to recognise the VIPs and who's-who of Italy – not an easy task for a young Australian fresh out of language school after just ten months in the country.

My next trip was a year later with my best friend, Stefano Miglio, by which time I was working for the fashion designer Enrico Coveri in Florence. That August, we headed south in my newly acquired, very second-hand Fiat 126, which looked like an old red jewellery box. This seemed like a good idea, until we hit the freeway and joined ten million other Italians heading south (here's a tip: don't attempt to drive around Italy in the month of August – the whole country goes on holidays and it's chaos!). Once in Positano, we set up base camp at a delightful *pensione* just outside town called La Fenice. The next day we arranged to meet some friends for lunch at a little beach restaurant they had recommended, where the food was delicious yet incredibly simple. We were told to wait on the jetty to the right of the main beach, where a small boat with a red wooden fish attached to its mast would pull up to take us over to Da Adolfo's, owned by Adolfo Bella. They also told us to be prepared to meet the best-looking boat boy on the coast, the owner's eldest son, Sergio. We were not disappointed – he was an Adonis! I fell in love with this boat boy, his boat, his coast, his food, his restaurant and even his family, and Sergio Bella and I became partners for the next eighteen years.

Everyone loved Sergio: the girls, the kids, the grandparents – even the other boys! He was drop-dead gorgeous, but calm and quiet (although he could erupt like Vesuvius when rubbed the wrong way). He was all the reason I needed to say goodbye to my fashion career in Florence and, six months after we met, I packed up my little red Fiat again and headed south to live with him in a tiny garage beneath the Bella family home in Positano. Those years were some of the happiest of my life.

Sergio had grown up at this little restaurant tucked away on Laurito beach, just five minutes by boat from Positano. His father, Adolfo, was, like most southern Italian fathers, tough on the outside and a big softie on the inside, and he presided over the organised chaos of the family business, giving each member of the family their own responsibilities. Sergio's American-born mother, Lucille, would be in the kitchen at dawn every day, making her magnificent American pies. Melania, Sergio's elder sister, worked the till and kept the customers in line with an icy stare when necessary. Sergio himself worked like a gladiator, setting up the tables every day, ferrying clients to and fro in the boat, and grilling the fish. Daniele, the youngest son, excelled in the kitchen from an early age. I have seen him work miracles over the years, crouched over the stove in the cave-like kitchen built into the mountain, regularly producing over 150 delicious meals in one sitting despite the temperature soaring to over 38 degrees (and it must have been over 40 degrees in the kitchen – no air conditioning in this neck of the woods!). His efficiency and speed were always impressive when he cooked for hungry crowds

in wet swimmers, who munched impatiently on crusty bread and sipped wine while they waited for their lunch. Although Daniele is based in Australia these days with his Australian wife, Nicole, and their kids, he often returns to Positano for the northern summer to cook at Da Adolfo's, and is never happier than when slaving over the hot stoves at the family restaurant. You can't take the Positano out of these men; it is embedded deep in their souls.

When I arrived in Positano, Sergio's father, Adolfo, had already been running Da Adolfo's for twenty years, and he still had another ten good years of fire left in him. He was a remarkable man in many ways, and took control of all the day-to-day aspects of running the restaurant. He decided when to make the wine, when to pick the myrtle berries, when to soak the lemon rind, when to stuff the squid, when to take the boat out for a day off work, when to paint the restaurant, and even when to play a prank on some poor unsuspecting victim (including me!). He became like a father to me, and over the years I spent a considerable amount of time with him, listening to magnificent tales of his exciting past, including his time as a courageous partisan with the Italian resistance in the northern hills of Italy, where his expertise in blowing up bridges was rewarded with a small shiny medal just before he passed away. He also loved to tell me how he came to discover his very own *piccolo paradiso*, Laurito Beach, where he would eventually set up the restaurant. He had always been passionate about the sea and anything to do with it, and this led him to team up with a friend in the 1950s and purchase a Riva speedboat, the very epitome of chic at the time, which they used to give tourists water-skiing lessons. A dream job for a young, attractive single man! It was on his many trips along the coast that he discovered the tiny sheltered cove where he would eventually open Da Adolfo's.

Adolfo always loved his animals, maybe more than he loved people. When I first met him, he had a huge white sheepdog called Zorba, who would sit between Adolfo's legs on the Vespa amongst his numerous shopping bags. When Zorba died, Adolfo was inconsolable – I had never seen him like that before. Zorba had been a permanent fixture in Adolfo's life and also in the town of Positano, which always seemed to have a resident 'character' dog. Back in the 1950s, it was a cocker spaniel called Vagliò (pronounced 'why yo') belonging to the local barber. Every afternoon the barber would give Vagliò a bag of soiled towels to take home for his wife to wash. The dog would carry the bundle in his mouth all the way home, and on arrival was promptly rewarded with dinner. When the small local bus service started up in the late 1950s, Vagliò quickly discovered he could take a short cut across town on the bus, and he did so until one day a 'No animals allowed' sign appeared on the bus windscreen. The locals were up in arms, and complained loudly to the authorities until Vagliò was reinstated. He continued to travel by bus (for free) until the day he died.

The Bella brothers, Sergio (above) and Daniele (below)

Baby Marco
with Melania Bella

A twelve-year-old Sergio standing in front of Da Adolfo's

Nicole and Daniele Bella

Adolfo Bella with Zorba

On my last visit with Adolfo before he died in early 2007, he looked fragile and thin. He was a very different man from the robust one I had met twenty-odd years before, who wore the earth on his skin and thought taking a dip in the sea was as good as scrubbing with soap under the shower. His skin was still the colour of warm chestnuts from years under the Mediterranean sun, and brought back memories of another nickname he was given by many enchanted foreign girls: the mahogany man. He was a true idealist and a champion of the masses – he never bowed to the rich and famous who would often visit his restaurant; instead he treated them just like everyone else, and they loved it. He was such an enormous presence in my life, and even today, when I am missing him, I set about preparing one of his favourite dishes, *pasta e lenticchie* (pasta with lentils) – the best comfort food I can think of.

Some things haven't changed since the early Da Adolfo years. A host of local boys still works the tables, running barefoot across the tiny hard pebbles of the beach, shouting orders and bolting up the twenty steps to the kitchen to bring back steaming bowls of pasta. Soon after moving to Positano, I became one of these running waiters, and I remember the work as some of the hardest I have ever done. But at the end of each day, when the last boatload of customers left, singing and laughing, for Positano, and the rest of the staff would stagger up the 400-odd steps to the road to their motorbikes and head home, the setting sun would embrace us with its warm rays and Sergio and I would swim in the crystal clear waters, drink chilled glasses of wine and cook juicy steaks on the embers of the grill still burning from the frantic day's work. Those were special times.

During my second summer working at the restaurant, my Italian step-brother, Nico (the son of my beloved Milanese stepfather Ettore Prossimo, who met my mother when I was just four and Nico fourteen), arrived from Sydney for a holiday. I was an established local by then, with good calluses on my feet from the pebbles, quads like a quarterback from running up and down the stairs for three hours a day, and vocal-cord nodes from yelling out orders. One day I dragged Nico out of his five-star hotel and begged him to help me at the restaurant – I was the only waiter working that day, it was the first busy weekend of the season and we were expecting big crowds as the weather was glorious. He couldn't refuse: Nico, like his father, had been in the restaurant game for decades, although I thought it might be a bit of a culture shock all the same. At the time, his inherited restaurant in Sydney, Donini's, was one of *the* up-market Italian establishments in the city, and catered to a decidedly elegant crowd. Da Adolfo's, on the other hand, was very southern Italian: relaxed, simple and slightly chaotic.

When Nico arrived with his white Panama hat propped on his head at just the right angle, and matching white linen pants and shirt, I had to stifle a giggle. Did he know he'd be running a grotty marathon within half an hour – sweating,

ABOVE: Adolfo on Laurito beach

BELOW: Maggie with Nico Prossimo

dusty and spattered with fish oil? Sure enough, the first boat arrived carrying about forty people, and the next three boats bought four times as many. It would be one hell of a day. But I could see Nico's eyes light up as he counted the customers and I could just hear him thinking, 'This is a gold mine!' I quickly showed him how to use the order pads, and told him, yes, you had to belt up twenty stairs to the kitchen for each and every order, slap the order down where Daniele could see it, grab a basket of bread and the oil and vinegar containers and fly back down the stairs, via the bar to pick up the wine and water – and just keep that up for a minimum of three hours. It was a real family day, with Adolfo at the till, Sergio by turns on the boat or behind the grill cooking the fish, Daniele in the kitchen, and Nico and me working the floor. We did a terrific job, and Nico was over the moon that we managed to serve 134 people, just the two of us, with not one complaint. Although Nico was paying well over $700 a night at his hotel back in town, I insisted on sharing our humble tips, and in the end he graciously accepted. When he put that 12,500 lira ($12 Australian) into his pocket, he patted it down proudly and said it was the best $12 he had ever earned. God bless my brother!

Over the years I met countless fascinating characters at the restaurant, regulars who would return year after year, just fitting in with the scenery like the pebbles on the beach. Eccentric characters have always been drawn to Da Adolfo's, and that's part of its enormous charm. In my early days as a waitress, one of our regulars was a renowned jeweller from Venice, who insisted she always sit at her favourite table. Although Da Adolfo's is, and always has been, a 'no reservations' restaurant, she felt it was *her* table, and if someone mistakenly put themselves there – well, there was hell to pay. In her early fifties, she was small yet formidable, and could be quite sharp when her order was not spot-on (especially with me, the new foreign waitress!). But the most amazing thing about her was that she would dine topless – all she would wear to lunch were her bikini bottoms, a deep tan and one of her selection of huge stone necklaces in amber, amethyst or turquoise. Her favourite table was on the terrace and fairly private, but she could still be seen by most diners, enjoying her meal in all her glory. All this was a non-event for the Italians, but was always a real eye-opener for the foreign guests.

Another regular, Cookie, was a New York journo for *Rolling Stone* magazine who never missed a beat or a summer at Da Adolfo's. She was an ex-girlfriend of Jimi Hendrix and totally looked the part: blonde hair with dark roots, tattoos, rings like knuckledusters on each finger, piercings in every conceivable part of her body way before it became fashionable, the tiniest bikinis in the world – and she was the greatest fun imaginable. She was a customer by day but she was our buddy by night, and we would wine and dine together as much as possible. Cookie was the only woman I have ever known who could walk around the Amalfi Coast at

ABOVE: A running waiter in action

BELOW: Cookie was a Da Adolfo regular

night in four-inch high stiletto heels – the sheer geography of the area does not usually allow for anything higher than a bedroom slipper.

When I first came to live in Positano, I was happy to help out in the restaurant for a while, as I'd just left a high-powered and often stressful fashion job in Florence (secretly I'd always wanted to be a waitress – all my friends had waited on tables after leaving school or during uni – and I was dying to have this experience, I knew I'd love it). But this work would not keep me occupied all year round, and I was keen to try my hand at something totally different. I soon saw that the tourist T-shirts sold locally were just awful and spotted a niche in the market, so I came up with a plan to design and print my own T-shirts. While back in Australia on holiday one year, I learnt the techniques of screen-printing from a dear friend of my mum Maggie's and one of the very best in the business, Ross Stay, the ex-head of East Sydney Technical College. I then set about researching suppliers of paints, screens and ovens, determined to do it all myself, from scratch. Unfortunately, most of these suppliers were in Naples, in a very dodgy area near the train station – not the safest spot for foreign blondes! Soon I set up a little studio in the spare room at Adolfo's house, and my first client was a small boutique down on the beach that made their own clothes and beachwear. The owner Virginia would provide unsewn fabric on which I would print my designs. My son, Marco, had just been born, so I spent my days furiously printing between breastfeeds, and then almost straight away I'd see my prints made into garments and hanging in her window. Soon after, Ross and I developed a very simple, bold, signature T-shirt design, which just sold and sold, and still does well today.

When Marco was barely a year old, my good friend Marcelo the Argentinean jeweller let me know that the little shop next door to his was vacant (shop leases are like needles in a haystack in Positano). I snapped it up and suddenly I was selling my T-shirts (as well as hand-painted shoes and hats) direct to the public. With summer approaching and rent on the shop to pay, I had to produce and sell a lot of stock – fast! With the help of family and friends, I managed to open my shop, Amanda Positano, within three weeks. I found an excellent T-shirt supplier just an hour's drive up the coast who made a top-quality T-shirt using a light cotton, and this became the canvas for my designs. It rained every day that June so the tourists had nothing to do but shop, and I sold a heap of T-shirts. Everyone loved them, although I felt they were pretty average to start with, but still better than what was out there! Soon I was able to buy my own screen-printing carousel and oven, by which time Sergio and I had moved out of the garage and into a tiny house just up the road from my new shop. Eventually the garage became my new printing studio, and life was perfect.

At the time, I had found a gem of a babysitter for Marco. Adriana, a petite 19-year-old fresh out of high school, had a real talent for getting him off to sleep.

ABOVE: **My T-shirt shop – open for business**

BELOW: **The signature T-shirt design that still sells today**

She would sit on the couch with him propped on her lap facing her, then wrap her arms around him tightly and rock him fiercely back and forth (and I mean a *really* hard rock – her little torso would shift 45 degrees back and forth). It was like nothing I had ever witnessed before, and Marco would drop off within minutes. Then she'd place him in the crib and set about watching him. Adriana would watch my baby boy for hours – this girl was dedication to the max. By the time I opened the T-shirt shop, Adri was my natural choice to run the store (I needed someone to watch my T-shirts with the same dedication she watched my baby!). In Adri's capable hands, the T-shirt shop continued to be a thriving business for the next ten years, while I searched for a new project to get my teeth into.

I had plans to create my own pure-linen collection of elegant, lightweight garments for men and women that would wear well in a hot climate. Through some good friends in the fashion business I soon found a wonderful supplier in the north of Italy that could produce high-quality dyed linens, and the Amanda Tabberer linen collection was born. This not only added a new look to my Positano T-shirt shop, it also became the foundation for the collection I import into Australia today. I would hold my fashion parades on the terrace of my good friend Monica Aonzo's beautiful Hotel Poseidon, featuring models of all nationalities selected from the expat community. Amongst the models from South Africa, India, Finland, Japan, France, the UK and Senegal was the odd Italian, and I even managed occasionally to persuade a famous friend or relative to participate, such as the actor David Keith (from *An Officer and a Gentleman*) or my mum, Maggie. What a nightmare it was trying to construct a bridge across the hotel pool sturdy enough for the models to walk across! But these parades were always a huge success, attracting attention both locally and in Naples, and helped to establish my boutique business and consolidate my existing T-shirt trade.

In the meantime we had upgraded from our tiny house near the shop to a larger one further up the mountain with the most breathtaking views of the village and the coast. The villa had five geranium-decked terraces and a balcony that projected out over the road. The only drawback we discovered was that snakes had taken up residence in the villa's lower level which had been vacant for a long time. Sergio assured me that, unlike Aussie snakes, these were harmless, and eventually they were eliminated (much to Marco's delight) with the purchase of two tabby cats, Jack and Jill.

Marco was living the life of a local boy, but with all the privileges of having his own little paradise – Da Adolfo's – down at Laurito beach. Typical of a Neapolitan boy, he went into business early. At the age of four he would draw abstract designs on unusual-shaped pebbles he picked off the beach, then lay them on a towel and sell them to our unsuspecting customers. He would eat lunch at Da Adolfo's every day during the warmer months, charging down the 350 stairs from his school to

ABOVE: Adri with baby Marco

BELOW: Marco at work creating his pebble designs

the jetty to jump on the last boat to Laurito, just in time for his pasta with clams. And during the long summer holidays when we were flat out working, he would simply squeeze between our legs on the Vespa to hitch a ride somewhere – to the beach, to a friend's place, to the soccer oval or to kayak lessons down the coast. It was a real-life fairytale.

Going to school in southern Italy does not present too many religious choices – so Roman Catholic it was for Marco. Sergio had been brought up a good Catholic boy, although I doubt he was the first in line at Sunday school each week. Marco, on the other hand, enjoyed going to church enormously, seeing it as a good chance to socialise and catch up with his mates (he would even spend time explaining religious philosophies to me – a committed atheist!). When it was time for his First Communion, I realised I had forgotten to have him baptised as a baby, so this was done in somewhat of a hurry a few weeks beforehand. Family and friends (and each of Marco's four babysitters) piled into the tiny church above Da Adolfo's for the formalities, then Sergio and I threw a beach party down below at the restaurant to seal the deal with God. Marco was beaming that day – but not as much as when he marched through town in his long, white robe, with 49 other boys and girls his age, on the day of his First Communion, in front of hundreds of teary-eyed relatives. And although I felt totally unfamiliar with this event, it was a wonderful experience to be part of.

As a family, we all led our own lives – Marco at school, Sergio in the restaurant and me at the shop – but we were always drawn together at that very special time of day in Italy: lunchtime. Whether it was at a quick bite at Da Adolfo's, a winter weekend feast in the mountains, or a long, late lunch at home, we would always try to share this meal together. We also loved to go on family boating trips, to fish for flying squid at night, or to dash to Nerano for an evening meal with visiting friends and family.

Having lived overseas since my late teens, I was used to being a long way from home, and by the time I fell in love with Sergio, moved to Positano and set up my business, I was too busy to dwell on this much – and anyway, I adored living in Italy. We usually managed to get back to Sydney for Christmas to see my family and friends and enjoy the surf at Bondi, and I always had plenty of visitors keen to spend time on the Amalfi Coast. My sister, Brooke, once came to visit and ended up staying three months – she has an artistic touch and was immediately put on hat-painting duty in my T-shirt shop. My stepbrother, Nico, would also come often, along with many of my other friends, but my mother, Maggie, was by far our most regular visitor. She loved the Amalfi Coast, and it was never hard to talk her into coming for a cuddle with her only grandson. She eventually became well known around Positano (almost as much as she is in Australia), and today there are very few local *Positanesi* who don't recognise her. As she walks down the street, they

ABOVE: Marco and I at his First Communion

BELOW: My sister Brooke helping out in the shop

14

call 'Madre Amanda! Ciao!', an amusing twist on the 'Oh, you must be Maggie's daughter!' that I get in Australia.

Adolfo had retired in the mid-1990s, handing over the business to Sergio. Daniele stayed on as head chef, Melania would occasionally lend a hand at the till, and Adolfo would appear now and then and pretend to run things. Much to the relief of the loyal established clientele, Sergio kept the *super simpatico* atmosphere of the restaurant alive and changed very little when he took over, except the wine list. He had been passionate for some time about wines from all over Italy, and the more exciting ones soon found their way into the cellar at Da Adolfo's. However, the spirit of Adolfo certainly lives on in this tiny cove, tucked away on the Amalfi Coast.

But even fairytales have to come to an end. Sergio and I went our separate ways after 18 years together in 2003. For many years we were considered the 'golden couple' of Positano, and although all endings are sad, I look back on our time together as a great success – we have many amazing memories, and best of all we have Marco. I decided to return to Australia so that Marco could complete his schooling here and I could establish my business interests. It was with mixed feelings that we left the magical town of Positano, but we were comforted by the fact that our return visits would be frequent – for Marco to visit his dad, and for me to continue my work and visit our cherished friends and our much-loved Amalfi coastline.

Almost from the moment I moved to Positano, family, friends and friends-of-friends would ask me for advice on where to stay, where to eat, what to see and how to get around the magnificent Amalfi Coast. As my knowledge of the area grew and I met more and more local people who ran wonderful restaurants, bars or hotels, I was able to make recommendations from my own first-hand experience. This inspired me to set up the villa rental business that I still run today. And after many years of providing this advice, I decided that writing a book might be an easier way (little did I know!). This was the catalyst for my return trip to Positano, and without the pressures of family and business to attend to, this time I was able to retrace my steps along the breathtaking coastline that I called home for so many years at my own pace, and to revel in the jewel-like villages, delicious food and wonderful people – those hardworking, passionate southern Italians. It's been an amazing journey, and by sharing it with you I hope to spread around a little of the magic of this wonderful place.

ABOVE: Marco working the Da Adolfo bar during his school holidays

BELOW: Back on my Amalfi coast

PASTA E LENTICCHIE (PASTA WITH LENTILS)

300 g brown lentils
2 tablespoons extra virgin olive oil
1 small brown onion, finely chopped
1 stick celery, finely chopped
1 carrot, finely chopped
1 potato, finely chopped

1 rind of parmesan
100 g Italian salami, sliced
salt
300 g mixed short pasta and spaghetti,
*   broken into short lengths*
grated parmesan, to serve

Rinse the lentils well in cold water. In a pressure cooker or large, heavy-based pan, add the olive oil, onion, celery, carrot, potato, parmesan rind, salami and lentils. Add salt to taste and cover with cold water by about 4 cm. Close the lid and bring to pressure if using a pressure cooker, otherwise cover and bring to a boil. Reduce heat to low and simmer for 45 minutes. (At this point, check the consistency of the stew – if it is very dense, add 1–2 cups water). Bring back to a boil, uncovered, and add the pasta. Cook for about 10 minutes, stirring continuously, until the pasta is cooked. Discard the parmesan rind, sprinkle over some grated parmesan and devour.

Serves 6

ADOLFO'S TOTANI RIPIENI (STUFFED FLYING SQUID)

extra virgin olive oil, for cooking
2 large cloves garlic, chopped
6 medium-sized raw squid
*   (approximately 1 kg), cleaned,*
*   tentacles removed and chopped*
salt

5–6 slices day-old ciabatta bread
¼ cup chopped flat-leaf parsley
100 g grated parmesan
6 toothpicks
2 x 400 g cans Italian tomatoes

Heat some olive oil in a frying pan, and sauté half the chopped garlic until golden. Add the chopped tentacles, cover and cook for 45 minutes, checking every 15 minutes or so and adding water if the mixture is drying out. Add salt to taste.

Tear the bread into small pieces and mix with the chopped parsley, parmesan and cooked tentacles. Fill each squid with this stuffing and close firmly with a toothpick. In a large, deep pan wide enough to hold all the squid in one layer, sauté the remaining chopped garlic in some olive oil. When golden, add the stuffed squid and sauté for 5 minutes. Add the tomatoes and cook, uncovered, on low–medium heat for 45 minutes or until tender.

Serves 2–3

POLLO ADOLFO (ADOLFO'S CHICKEN)

6 x chicken marylands
   (leg and thigh portions)
1/3 cup dried black olives
2 sprigs fresh rosemary, leaves chopped
1 kg red pontiac or other waxy potatoes,
   cut into 2 cm cubes

1 large brown onion, finely sliced
250 ml dry white wine
salt, to taste
a splash of extra virgin olive oil

Preheat the oven to 220°C. Place all the ingredients in a large baking dish, pour over 250 ml water and cook for 30 minutes. Reduce the oven temperature to 180°C and cook, regularly basting the meat with the pan juices, for a further hour or until the chicken is cooked all the way through. (Add more water to the pan if the juices dry out too much.)
Serves 6

DANIELE'S PEACH CROSTATA

250 g strong plain flour (such as
   Italian '00')
125 g sugar

125 g butter, at room temperature,
   chopped
1 egg, plus an extra yolk
500 g fresh peaches, sliced

Tip the flour onto a clean workbench and mix with the sugar. Rub in the butter with your fingers to combine. Make a well in the centre and add the egg and extra egg yolk. Mix with two fingers until the yolks break, then lightly knead the ingredients together (do not overwork the pastry or it will crumble). Form into a large ball, wrap in plastic film and place in the fridge for a couple of hours.

   Preheat the oven to 180°C. When required, roll the pastry out thinly into a rectangular shape. Arrange the peach slices in the middle, leaving a 2 cm border, then fold the edges in to form a crust. Sprinkle with some extra sugar, and bake for 30–40 minutes, or until the crust is golden.

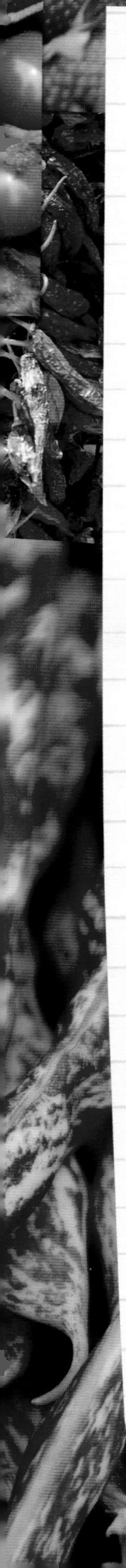

Recipes reproduced with the kind permission of Daniele Bella.

2 AMALFI
6 MINORI
7 MAIORI
8 RAVELLO
ILARIA TI AMO
17 ↑ CETARA
PIMONTE → MicHeLe
BEATRICE
22 ROSARIA VIETRI
01-03-06

POSITANO, *LA CITTÀ ROMANTICA* (THE CITY OF ROMANCE) POPULATION: Officially 3900, but swells to 10000 during the summer months INHABITANTS: *Positanesi* ORIGINS OF THE NAME: There are plenty of theories, so take your pick: (1) Positano may be derived from the name of the Greek sea god, Poseidon; (2) the town may have taken its name from Posides, a former slave from the time of Emperor Tiberius, who built a number of luxury villas in the area, most likely including the Roman villa along the main beach which is currently being excavated; (3) the ancient Pasitea (Positano) may have been a Greek settlement, if so, it is possible that the name

came from *posa tanos*, meaning sloping land; (4) the name may have come from Paestum, an ancient town whose inhabitants fled along the coast to seek refuge from invading aggressors **DISTRICTS:** Montepertuso, Nocelle, Laurito **PATRON SAINT:** San Vito, protector of the dancer, celebrated on 15 June **MOTHER CHURCH (*CHIESA MADRE*):** Santa Maria Assunta **TOWERS:** Sponda, Trasita and Fornillo **TYPICAL DISH:** *Totani fritti* (fried flying squid), an ancient dish prepared by the fishermen of this town; glazed with egg and fried until golden, this is a favourite dish to serve at festivals and celebrations

'FLAMING LIKE A METEOR WE HIT THE COAST, A ROAD, HIGH, HIGH ABOVE THE BLUE SEA, THAT HOOKED AND CORKSCREWED ON THE EDGE OF NOTHING... IN THE BACK SEAT MY WIFE AND I LAY CLUTCHED IN EACH OTHER'S ARMS, WEEPING HYSTERICALLY...'

JOHN STEINBECK, ON ARRIVING IN POSITANO

A FAMILIAR BEAUTY

Positano grips a magnificent stretch of rocky, curving coastline through which the main road winds perilously close to the cliff-edge. This must be the most photographed town on the Amalfi Coast – its panorama of chalk-white Moorish-style buildings (with the occasional gelato-coloured one to break the monotony) is recognised worldwide. And the contrasting deep-blue of the Mediterranean Sea that embraces this town gives a perfect aesthetic balance. Surrounded by the magnificent Lattari Mountains, Positano has been built on the most dramatic cliff face on the coastline. Its concentration of rooftops huddled tightly together, seemingly stacked one on top of the other, create a pyramid shape that when viewed from the sea resembles an arrowhead pointing to the sky.

Much of the architecture in Positano, and all along the Amalfi Coast, features the classic Mediterranean/Arabic cupola-shaped tiled dome. *Chiesa Madre* (right), the magnificent mother church of Positano, is covered in beautiful sea-green, lemon-yellow, black and white majolica tiles, the famous enamelled tiles originally from Majorca in Spain. These coloured tiles appear to be something of a trade-mark amongst churches up and down the Amalfi Coast, which can often prove disorientating for visitors – especially when buying postcards. Over the years I have seen countless postcards featuring churches with the wrong town written in the caption, such is their similarity.

The *pistrice* is a legendary mythical creature, half fish, half dragon, that has become a symbol of Positano, representing the town and its mysterious mythology for centuries. The creature is depicted on a beautiful medieval bas-relief (above) on the main bell tower of the *Chiesa Madre*, neatly placed above the entrance. Some say this creature characterises the blend of land and sea activities of the town. In fact, the villagers often joke in a slightly contemptuous way about the *montanaro* (mountain dwellers), who live so close to the sea but are unable to even swim! From what I have seen, the *montanaro* are not the slightest bit interested – they love their land and mountains and rarely bother to come down to the more touristy seaside.

BEGINNINGS

Like many places in this area, the origins of Positano have become a mix of fact and fiction, history and legend. The Greeks and Phoenicians most likely visited this area first as they travelled west many centuries ago. During the time of the Roman Empire, Positano served an important purpose for the emperor Tiberius, exiled on the nearby island of Capri. He believed the masses despised him so much that they wanted him dead, so he would send his men up the coast to Positano to obtain 'safe' flour to bake his bread. Positano was also a popular holiday spot for the nobles of the time, evidenced by the ruins of a Roman villa on the Galli Islands, just a few kilometres offshore from Positano, and recent archaeological discoveries of another magnificent villa beneath the town, that was most likely covered with ash from the eruption of Mount Vesuvius in 79 AD.

With the fall of the Roman Empire, Positano became a part of the independent Maritime Republic of Amalfi, that soon accumulated great wealth through its burgeoning trade with other countries in the Mediterranean. The affluence of the *Positanese* brought attacks from pirates and neighbouring states, and by the fifteenth century, the town had fortified itself with three magnificent protective towers.

For over two centuries, Positano enjoyed a reputation as one of the great boat-building regions of the country. It was called the Golden Mountain as it was the richest area within reach of Naples, and by the 1700s was also known as a *regia citta* (director city) for its importance in the south. It was around this time that the wonderful baroque villas, many of them still standing today, were built into the side of the mountain and furnished with great treasures bought back from all over the world.

The unification of Italy in the mid-nineteenth century forced large numbers of *Positanese* to migrate to America, many of whom ended up in the heart of New York City, where they set up life *alla Positanese* – Positano-style. Today, there are more *Positanese* living in New York than there are in Positano. At the start of the twentieth century, the era of the Grand Tour, travellers from all over the world started to disembark on these shores. At the end of World War II, many of the American and English servicemen who had spent time in this area returned home singing the praises of its beauty and serenity – and the word was out. Modern-day tourism soon arrived in Positano, with a massive influx of overseas visitors in the 1950s and 1960s cementing the town's status as one of the world's most popular holiday destinations.

FAMOUS FACES

Positano has long been a magnet for the cognoscenti and glitterati from all over the world. In the early 1920s and '30s, the town harboured such important figures as renowned writers Misha Semenov and Essad Bey, the architect and writer Gilbert Clavel, the Dutch graphic artist M.C. Escher and the well-known Polish ceramicist and fabric designer Irene Kowaliska. The immense beauty of the landscape and the relative isolation of the town at this time made it a haven of peace and tranquillity for these creative souls.

Later, as Positano's popularity grew, many writers, artists and film directors visited this magical coastline, and some chose to stay and make their home here. The town attracted names like Henri Matisse, Ernest Hemingway, John Steinbeck, Franco Zeffirelli, Rudolf Nureyev, Eduardo de Filippo and Roberto Rossellini, plus scores of other famous movie stars and musicians, all of whom have helped to put Positano on the map.

APPROACHING POSITANO

There are three ways to get to Positano. Firstly, by boat – but only when seas are calm. Secondly, by road – which most people choose, and then they reach the hundredth bend and begin to wish they had come by boat! Your last option is to come by helicopter – but this is usually reserved for billionaires and politicians.

Whichever way you look at it, Positano is not an easy destination to reach, but once you arrive, the beauty of this small seaside town makes it all worthwhile. (And many people see the difficult access as a good thing, helping to keep the 'riffraff' and daytrippers out!) This former fishing village, which didn't even have electricity until 1933, now boasts over forty restaurants, sixty-odd hotels and *pensioni*, and somewhere between two and three thousand beach beds. In addition, countless apartments and villas are available for holiday rental.

If you are coming to Positano from the north on the A3 freeway (from Rome or Naples), take the exit for Castellammare, 27 kilometres from Naples. This takes you past Sorrento to the Positano end of the Amalfi Coast and involves a long 10 minutes of nail-biting hairpin bends (but you do get to marvel at the stunning views of the Mediterranean Sea along the way). If you miss the turn-off for Castellammare, you'll need to drive for another half hour or so until you reach Vietri sul Mare, just before Salerno. There you'll see a sign to the Amalfi Coast – take it, or you will end up in Sicily! This entails a 36-kilometre drive back along the Amalfi Coast road to Positano – an hour of hairpin bends, but again, one of the most spectacular coastal drives in the world.

THE SITA BUS

SITA buses are an essential part of life along the Amalfi Coast. The drivers know this stretch of road better than anyone, and although arrival and departure times can be a little unpredictable, you are sure to reach your destination in the end. I have seen foreign bus drivers, whose large vehicles are stuck on impossible corners, sitting by the side of the road weeping with frustration. In these situations, it's often a SITA bus driver who saves the day by taking the foreign beast by its wheel and coaxing it out of its tight corner. The show is always a good one, after which Signor SITA bows generously at cheering crowds in overheated cars before returning to his bus. The locals have no patience with foreign buses that clog up their route, and *adore* the SITA drivers who make it work again. The SITA buses belt along at an incredible speed, but if the road allows, the driver will always pull over to let cars pass. Foreign bus drivers, on the other hand, rarely extend this courtesy, not considering the nail-biting frustration of being stuck behind a slow, smelly bus for 30–60 minutes of hairpin bends.

THE COASTAL ROAD

Construction of the Amalfi Coast road began in 1816 and was finished forty-odd years later – it was not an easy feat! Although the road made the coast more accessible to travellers, the area still remained reasonably isolated for the first half of the twentieth century, when artists, composers, writers, poets and intellectuals flocked there, attracted by its remote beauty and seclusion. The cliff-clinging coastal road, today called the SS 163, is also known as the Nastro Azzurro (Blue Ribbon) for the sparkling Mediterranean Sea and endless sky that are visible from every curve along this 40-kilometre stretch of road.

LA CHIESA NUOVA

Arriving in Positano by road, La Chiesa Nuova is the first busy area you will come to. Just beneath the church of the same name is **Bar Internazionale**, the local pulse of Positano.

This is not a glamorous bar but a meeting spot for locals and tourists alike. The coffee and pastries smell dangerously good and there are always half a dozen civil servants leaning up against the bar, replenishing their strength to cope with demanding members of the public who come to them to report this loss, that renewal or those problems. This is how the public servants of Italy deal with unsavoury matters: over a good chat and a coffee.

You will hear the name Bar Internazionale over and over again if you are visiting Positano. Everything seems to happen here and without it the business life of the town would surely grind to a halt. The big buses from Rome, Naples and Sorrento stop here, as does the little local bus that circumnavigates Positano day and night. You can have a snack or a pizza, linger over a cocktail, or buy anything from delicious Easter eggs to expensive bottles of wine and sometimes the works of local artists. You can also go online, check your post and fill in your lottery forms. The locals leave messages, money and packages for friends or business colleagues with Mimi, the owner. The bar also acts as a rendezvous point for all the young kids on their motorbikes and cars who are heading off to Sorrento in one direction or Amalfi in the other. It is where locals meet for coffee to discuss politics or family issues, crowding together to share the five tables and benches. Early in the morning the local construction workers meet here for breakfast, and late-night stragglers often end up here for a last drink.

On Sunday mornings, all the bars along the Amalfi Coast are like international food fairs and, with its own pastry kitchen next door, Bar Internazionale is no exception. You will often see Virginia manoeuvring huge trays of fresh pastries from the kitchen to the bar amid passing buses, tourists loaded with rucksacks, and rows of parked motorbikes. Large platters and boxes of *dolce* (sweets and desserts) are piled high, especially in winter, when the locals have more time to stop and eat. This is an important pit stop on Sunday mornings to buy dessert to accompany a delicious home-cooked Sunday lunch.

Il Grottino Azzurro, next door to Bar Internazionale, is one of the first restaurants I ate at in Positano, twenty-three years ago. Raffaele and Concetta have been running this simple family business for over twenty-five years (they do the cooking while their sons wait the tables). Raffa does the best baked fish in white wine I've ever tasted. When you come here you are practically eating in the middle of the road at a bus stop. People pull up on their Vespas to say hello, or just sit themselves down at the table for a chat or glass of wine, so it's easy to while away

OPPOSITE: The simple stylised dome of the *Chiesa Nuova*; making pasta in the closet-sized kitchen at Il Grottino Azzurro; Virginia in the well-stocked Bar Internazionale

an entire afternoon there. And like Bar Internazionale, Il Grottino has local artists' work on the walls that are sometimes for sale.

Two large photographic collages hang at one end of the small dining room. They are the work of my clever friend Jenny Hanlon, an Aussie expat who has been living in Positano for years. The collages represent nearly every local and foreign friend of this restaurant from the last couple of decades. There's a picture of me on my beaten-up old bike with my tiny three-year-old son Marco sandwiched between my legs in the way that most small kids ride with their parents in this town. Memories flood over me as my eye wanders around this incredible array of familiar faces. Eighteen years of my life here on this one restaurant wall!

Further along the street you will find the best *pescheria* (fish shop) in town, **Pescheria Pasquale de Lucia**. Pasquale and his three good-looking sons operate this demanding business, often supplying the top hotels in the area. If you are planning to cook your own fish while staying in Positano, make sure you buy in the morning when the produce is abundant and fresh. But don't expect row upon row of anonymous fillets. The fish are whole, and Pasquale will scale and gut, and probably fillet as well, although in the eighteen years I lived there I never asked him to, because locals firmly believe that filleting is the best way to lose all the fine and subtle flavours of the fish.

Pasquale generally has a good choice of crustaceans, including *scampi* (a prawn-like shellfish) and tiny fresh prawns you don't even need to peel – just eat them, shell and all. Naturally his *vongole* (baby clams) are always *senza* sand (well-cleaned) and delicious, and when in season his mussels are plump and excellent.

Just down the road from the fish shop is a traditional butcher, **Sirocco's Macelleria**, where you will find excellent local meats. I would always buy half a small goat from Sirocco's at Easter time to be marinated overnight in olive oil, white wine and rosemary, before being roasted over burning coals and served with seasonal vegetables – a traditional Easter lunch. They also have a great selection of local pork, rabbit and turkey.

MONTEPERTUSO

I think of Montepertuso, a district of Positano three kilometres straight up the mountain, as a little fairy village. It has just one grocer, one church, and in typical southern Italian style, one professional-size soccer field and four restaurants.

Il Ritrovo is one of my favourite mountain restaurants. You just have to make sure you are good and hungry, as the portions are generous. The owner Salvatore has an excellent selection of wines to complement his food. I suggest you head up the mountain on foot to build up your appetite, or if you can't bear the thought, bus or taxi it up and then wander gently back down as a good digestive.

CLIMB OR SLIDE
The one essential requirement for visiting the Amalfi Coast is to have working (or walking) legs – this is not a wheelchair-friendly holiday destination! The numerous stone staircases offer shortcuts up, down and around town. As John Steinbeck famously said in a captivating account of his visit here in the 1950s, published in *Harpers Bazaar*, 'You do not walk to visit a friend [in Positano], you either climb or slide.'

Taking the stairs will always cut off a few curves and get you where you want to go faster, but they can be heart-attack material, especially in the midday sun. My view is if you are going down, cut through the curves of town by using the stairs (you will see them everywhere), but if you are hiking up, use the road – it's much gentler.

OPPOSITE: Marco and I in Jenny Hanlon's famous collage on the walls of Il Grottino Azzurro (top middle); Raffa and his son await the lunch crowd at Il Grottino Azzurro (top left); handsome Pasquale tosses shiny fresh mussels in seawater for the morning sales (below left)

THE LEGEND OF MONTEPERTUSO

Montepertuso means 'hole in the mountain' in the local dialect, and as the bus takes you up the narrow windy road from Positano, you'll see the dramatic, oval-shaped hole (above) in the rock that gives the town its name. The legend goes that the Madonna and the Devil met while walking in the woods, and he challenged the Madonna to create a hole in the rock. The Devil had tried repeatedly without success, but the Madonna simply touched the rock and it crumbled away.

I love this legend, and it is celebrated every 2 July with the very popular Festa della Madonna. A statue of the Madonna is marched ceremoniously around the town in a religious procession, then carried up to the hole in the mountain. A massive fireworks display erupts, which has been known to set the mountain on fire – the locals are always prepared though, standing by with sand and water to extinguish the flames. The festival is cancelled when the winds are too strong, but in my eighteen years on the coast, this happened only once – it has to be blowing a serious gale to stop this festival. If you are in Positano at this time of year, make sure you get the bus up to Montepertuso for this wonderful celebration, and book one of the local restaurants for dinner.

Salvatore preserves his own tomatoes to use throughout the winter – called *piennoli*, he hangs them from the restaurant ceiling at the end of summer. These cherry-sized tomatoes contain their own preservatives and, if they are not over-watered when on the vine, they won't rot when dried. They are sweet yet salty, just like a tomato should be, and totally delicious. They make the very best sautéed tomato sauces and are used in the traditional dish *la pasta con o'pesc' fujit* (pasta with the fish that got away), a simple tomato sauce made with garlic and basil, where the saltiness of the tomatoes gives a suggestion of the sea. You will see these bunches of small round tomatoes hanging in shops and kitchens up and down the coast from the end of summer and all through winter. They are an essential part of life here.

Salvatore works wonders in the kitchen and his partner in love and life, Teresa, runs the place with great efficiency, but she is a big softy, and makes the best homemade cookies I've ever eaten, which she generously scatters around the liqueurs tray at the end of the meal. Salvatore makes an array of delicious and deadly liqueurs. His *limoncello* is a must, but he also makes other wonderful flavours like basil, strawberry, hazelnut and aniseed. If you're looking to learn more about Salvatore's secrets, try his rustic cooking classes (held in the low season only).

Another wonderful Montepertuso restaurant – and one for a really special meal – is **Donna Rosa**. Enzo, the owner, is always on hand to offer a special wine and a mouth-watering description of what Raffaela, his wife, has cooked that evening. My Italian-born stepbrother Nico claims he had one of the best meals of his life in this restaurant (and he has eaten plenty all over the world): baked cod with clams and peas. It's also one of my favourite meals – it's rarely on the menu but they often seem to have it if you ask. Enzo explained to me years ago that when they buy their cod they always check if the fish have been caught with a net or a hook. They prefer the hook-caught ones as they are fresher and will not have been hanging around in the nets all night. Cod must be eaten very fresh, Raffaele says, as it makes a big difference to the flavour. Enzo once told me the story of offering this dish to Neapolitan guests, and their response was, 'Why? Do I look sick?' Apparently Neapolitans associate cod with food you eat when you are unwell!

NOCELLE

This precious little hilltop village, with just one bar, one deli and one restaurant, was always a favourite of Adolfo's. He would often bring the whole family up here to simply sit on someone's roof and admire the spectacular view of the sea below. Today the local bus travels up the windy road from Montepertuso a few times a day to allow visitors to enjoy one of the most spectacular vistas on the coast. Although the town is now scattered with villas available to rent, you always have a wonderful feeling of being totally isolated and away from the madding crowd.

OPPOSITE: **A proud mountain face,** Raffaele Casola of Nocelle

The famous Walk of the Gods that starts in Praiano ends here in Nocelle with a well deserved home-cooked meal at **Santa Croce** restaurant, which also has jaw-dropping views. They do a fabulous rabbit dish and jumbo-sized baked potato chips (from potatoes grown in their own garden) – delicious!

FESTIVAL OF THE FISH

It's a good idea to pass by the tourist information office soon after you arrive in Positano to find out if there are any town fairs, concerts or special events on. My favourite is the Sagra del Pesce (Festival of the Fish), which runs during the last week in September at Fornillo Beach, near Positano's main beach. This festival had been a regular one for most of my eighteen years in Positano, but suddenly fell by the wayside as it required too much voluntary work and everyone in town was either too busy at the end of summer or just too tired to help. However, it seems that five years on, it has been reinstated with gusto.

One year, my great buddy Bibi and I wandered down to the festival at sunset. All up and down the beach there were queues of people with tickets in hand waiting to be served a range of typical fish dishes, including *pasta e totani* (flying squid with short pasta), *la frittura* (fried fish) and *totani e patate* (flying squid stew with potatoes). There were also loads of people being dropped off by boat from the main beach. The atmosphere was like a welcome-home party, with everyone embracing and smiling broadly.

By the time night fell, our bellies were full and the atmosphere was pumping. The mayor, Domenico Marrone, had organised a Neapolitan folk group, Damacala, to entertain us. The five male falsetto voices and two sexy gypsy-like female dancers had us captivated. Domenico was the first one up on the wooden dance floor that had been laid on the sand earlier that day. Not long after, local icon Gianni Menichetti was up and dancing too. Tuscan-born Gianni is always dressed in vibrant colours and his face is heavily but beautifully tattooed. Whenever there is a local festival with music you will find this delightful artist dancing in the middle of the throng. He and long-time partner, eccentric Australian artist Vali Myers, were always present at musical festivals up and down the coast. Vali has since passed away, but Gianni continues the tradition and dances alone or with anyone who'll join him on the dance floor.

The band finished with an interpretation of the ancient Neapolitan dance performed by two men, with two of their legs entwined, hopping energetically on their other leg. Exhausted, they left the large crowds applauding and begging for more.

While all this was going on, the local fishermen had thrown a massive net out to sea and after hauling it in, fried up the catch to feed the hungry revellers. It was a truly magical night.

OPPOSITE: Artist and colourful local Gianni Menichetti and scenes from one of the many summer festivals

FERRAGOSTO

The patron saint of Positano is officially San Vito (whose day is celebrated on 15 June), but Maria Assunta is the name given to the town's main church, and it is she who is celebrated with great enthusiasm on 15 August (Ferragosto). The entire country is also on holiday that day to celebrate the middle of summer, and almost everything is closed, even in seaside tourist destinations along the Amalfi Coast (except restaurants, of course – the Italians have to eat!). On this day Positano is one big open-air festival, with spectacular fireworks launched from a large barge just off the main beach. Every balcony, terrace, restaurant and street that faces the sea is packed with tourists and locals alike, all of them angling for the best view of the fireworks. And the sea is alive with hundreds of boats jostling for a good position.

For years Sergio and I would brave the watery chaos on Ferragosto. We would putter along the coast from Laurito in the pitch dark towards the main beach in our own little boat to enjoy this unique event. Our evening was spent with some good cheese, bread and wine on board our little vessel bobbing on the sea. Sergio always knew where to anchor for the best view – and naturally had the quickest getaway when it was all over. We would make a dash back to Laurito before the other boats even had their anchors off the sea floor.

OTHER KEY EVENTS IN POSITANO

SAGRA DELLO ZEPPOLA (Fried Sweet Dough Festival) – celebrated around Christmas time, this festival is loved by kids and adults alike. It lasts for three days, with soccer competitions on the beach, street stalls, hot sausage sandwiches and pizzas, and a prize for the best *zeppola*.

PREMIO DELLA DANZA (Dance Awards) – this has been around for over fifty years, and is probably the town's most well known and established international event. On the first Saturday of September, dancers from all over the world gather to compete on an enormous stage on the main beach of Positano. This event is dedicated to the famous Russian ballet dancer, Leonide Massine.

QUATIERE APERTO (Open Quarters) – held from the end of August right through to December. Other towns from all over the region of Campania are invited to Positano to share their legends, their music and culture, and to sell their handcrafted wares from quaint little wooden stalls scattered throughout the town.

SAN PIETRO – Although San Pietro is not a Positano saint, the magnificent five-star hotel of the same name celebrates 29 June regardless, with a street fair and impressive fireworks.

MARE SOLE E CULTURA (Sea, Sun and Culture) – this takes place during the long hot summer months. Amongst other things, famous Italian and international writers gather in Positano to launch their latest works.

POSITALIA – **Hotel Palazzo Murat** hosts classical music concerts in their magnificent gardens on the way down to the beach. These are generally held at sunset.

40

A CURE FOR JET LAG, POSITANO-STYLE

Late one summer my cousin Michelle came to stay with me in Positano. She arrived from Brisbane on a Saturday night, so I thought I'd better get her out onto the local dance floor straight away before her jet lag could kick in. **Music on the Rocks**, the only nightclub in town, would soon be closing for the winter months, but luckily Mish had arrived just in time to enjoy a night at this classic, unique disco. (If you are after a disco vacation, make sure you come to Positano right in the middle of the northern summer during July and August, not at the very end or beginning.)

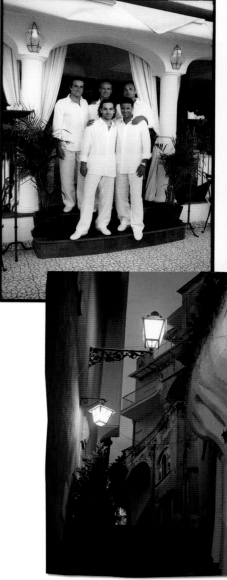

But first we kicked off the night upstairs at the very elegant **Le Terrazze** restaurant, owned and run by the nightclub owner Peppino Russo. Mish was in awe of the olive-skinned, dark-eyed young Italians with slick smooth hair and *Vogue Uomo* looks (right). Peppino must have hand-picked them like good grapes!

After dinner we headed downstairs to the nightclub. I love these discos in Italy. It doesn't matter what age you are, you simply sit there, tap your feet in time to the music and you can be sure that sooner or later, some charming young Italian will ask you to dance. We had a few dances then at 2 a.m. struggled up the treacherous staircase known as La Scalinatella – a marathon of approximately 350 steps – that connects the main beach with Punta Reginella, the area of my apartment and the lovely **Hotel Poseidon**. I call this the emergency route. If you are so tired that a gentle stroll up through town is not an option, you just need to take the shortest way home and tough it out up the stairs. After I subjected Mish to the marathon climb she was asleep before her head hit the pillow – a twenty-six-hour flight, a four-hour train and taxi trip from Rome to Positano, then straight out for dinner and dancing. I felt cruel, but I knew it would be good for her jet lag – she wouldn't have any!

EATING AND DRINKING

Another late-night entertainment spot in Positano also happens to offer some of the best breakfast treats in town. Surrounded by lush citrus orchards, **La Zagara Bar** (The Orange Blossom Bar) is well known for its night-time entertainment during the summer months. Nello Buongiorno sings old favourites into the wee hours while playing his electric piano, which makes more sounds than a ten-piece band. Nello woos people onto the small dance floor with every possible style of music. A favourite with the older generations, it has a great retro/karaoke feel that also appeals to the young. You can't miss the Zagara when you walk down to the beach; its window display is stuffed with every creamy, puffy, sugary, yummy pastry you could imagine. The red-vested waiters take you back to another era and are utterly charming.

Of course, my favourite restaurant of all in Positano has to be **Da Adolfo's**. Here are my picks for their must-try dishes:

- mozzarella grilled on a lemon leaf (but don't eat the lemon leaf – it's for flavour and perfume, not roughage!)

- *alici marinate* (small marinated anchovies), soaked in just enough vinegar to give them a tangy bite, but not too much that the flavour is overpowering

- any whole grilled fish, but the *bandiera* (ribbon), with very few bones and a great flavour, is a particular favourite of mine; the mint dressing served with it is sublime

- Daniele's *crostata*, a pie with a hard crust topped with fresh peaches, plums, strawberries or whatever is in season (some customers have been known to order a corner piece as soon as they arrive, so they don't miss out on that delicious crust)

The luxury five-star hotel **Il San Pietro** has one of the best views of Positano, where you can gaze back at the pyramid of lolly-coloured houses from just two kilometres up the coast. Carlo and Vito Cinque, with their mother, Virginia, are the owners of this iconic hotel. Its quiet and relaxed ambience attracts many international celebrities who return year after year. Il San Pietro offers something elite and luxurious but without the fuss and pomp of many upmarket establishments.

Carlo and Vito's great uncle Carlo 'Carlino' Cinque started to build the little outcrop of rooms in the early '60s, eventually opening thirty-odd rooms to mostly acquaintances. Today the number of rooms has doubled but the exclusive atmosphere remains. Sergio's cousin Salvatore Bella has worked the bar in this hotel for years and makes one of the most exquisite bellini cocktails (made from fresh peach juice and *prosecco*, a sparkling Italian white wine) I have ever had. If you can't afford to stay or eat at Il San Pietro, consider at least enjoying a sunset cocktail on the terrace.

Another fabulous spot for an early evening cocktail is the bar at the up-market **Le Sirenuse** hotel, where you can indulge in champagne and oysters, and relax in the kasbah-style surroundings.

During my first few years in Positano, Sergio would often take me to Osteria O'Capurale, with its contemporary, frescoed ceiling (below left). We ate simple, tasty bowls of homemade pasta with beans or chickpeas. I have known the owners, Angela and Matteo (who was Marco's soccer coach), for years. Angela's grandmother was a mountain farmer who started this business back in the early 1950s, and in 1957, when the restaurant was an established success, she commissioned the great local German artist Michele Thiele to paint the main dining room ceiling. He created a fascinating masterpiece of the daily toils and hardships of the local fishermen's lives. I love it – it is so seaside Italian!

O'Capurale served honest wholesome dishes. Like many restaurants up and down the coast, the kitchen staff came from one of the Lattari Mountain villages and they were all great cooks. Classic *paesano* (rustic) dishes they served were: *gateau di patate* (potato bake); *broccoli con vongole* (broccoli and baby clam pasta); and *paccheri con pomodorini, rughetta, gorgonzola e gamberetti* (pasta with baby tomatoes, rocket, gorgonzola and baby prawns). This last dish was a favourite of Matteo's, who always had a healthy stock of good gorgonzola to hand. O'Capurale was a truly seasonal restaurant, closing from the end of October until the following Easter.

When I first opened my T-shirt shop, a man called Bruno used to run the little bar next door. I think Bruno regularly cleaned out his espresso machine with salt, as many barmen did in those days, and my cappuccino often had a salty edge. He sold the usual bar nuts, chips and lollies – nothing elaborate. It was one of the

OPPOSITE: Sunning, snacking, swimming or getting married – there is plenty to do on the famous rocky terrace of Il San Pietro

less exciting bars in town, but boasted the best views, overlooking the main beach and town, and near Le Sirenuse hotel. Today it is run by one of Bruno's daughters, Ornella, along with her clever chef husband Mario. The food is terrific, especially the *linguine con scorfano o cuoccio* (linguine with delicate pieces of deep-sea fish). In fact, the whole experience is memorable: you eat well-priced, fabulous food at small tables on a slanted footpath with a gorgeous view. Truly a romantic night out. And these days, there's not a hint of salt in the coffee.

NERANO

Nerano is a fabulous spot for lunch and is just 50 minutes from Positano by boat. The choice of restaurants on this tiny stretch of beach is so vast it's almost embarrassing! To get there, you can rent your own boat from any of the boat hire places on the main beach.

One of the best restaurants to visit in Nerano is **Ristorante il Cantuccio**. Here, they serve antipasti that go for kilometres and arrive at the table almost before your bottom hits the seat! In all my visits there over the years, I have rarely managed to get past this course, although in recent times, the beautiful and exotic owner Giovanna (left) has tapered down the quantity of dishes at my request – so I can at least get to the pasta and the wonderful fish they serve after. Nerano is famous for its zucchini pasta, and Giovanna does a particularly light and tasty one which I love. After a short, strong espresso, you can flop back onto the soft boat cushions to be driven lazily back along the coast to Positano. I have been making this day trip for twenty years, and it is never a disappointment – I can highly recommend it.

Other great eats in or near Nerano are:

- **Conca del Sogno** (top right) is in Recommone, the bay you reach just before you get to Nerano. The restaurant is made up of large open-air terraces and offers a sophisticated menu. Anna runs this restaurant brilliantly, attending to locals, tourists and a host of well known Italian celebrities (and their boats).

- **Taverna del Capitano** is a restaurant that also has a few rooms to rent and is just a few doors up from Il Cantuccio. The rooms are reasonably priced, but the menu is very sophisticated, so make sure you take your credit card.

- **Ristorante Maria Grazia**, with its white-washed wooden terrace, is probably one of the most famous restaurants on this beach. They, too, are famous for their zucchini pasta (but I personally prefer the lighter version next door). I like the atmosphere in this restaurant; it is very Mediterranean (sometimes the staff are nice, and other times they can be a little chilly!).

ABOVE: Bruno resting outside Bar Bruno after the busy lunch trade has gone home for a siesta

51

SLOW FOOD ON THE AMALFI COAST

In 1986 the Slow Food movement was founded in northern Italy by Carlo Petrini, a well-known writer horrified by the increasing number of fast food outlets opening up around the country. The movement was consolidated in Paris in 1989, when fifteen countries gave their support to its aims. The Slow Food philosophy focuses on the relaxed enjoyment of wholesome local, seasonal foods that have been carefully produced, keeping the sustainability of the environment in mind.

The Slow Food movement in Italy has grown enormously over the last two decades and its annual guidebook walks you through a large array of excellent eateries and restaurants throughout Italy. There is a price limit too – a restaurant could have the best wine and food in the world, but if the price is extortionate, you won't find them in the book. Sergio and I used this guide for years on our travels and it was always spot on.

In 1999, Cittaslow (Slow Cities or Slow Towns) were established to promote a way of life that supports good eating habits. To be accredited Slow City status, settlements must have fewer than 55 000 inhabitants and meet certain criteria regarding noise, sewage, and car use as well as the harmony maintained between the place and its surroundings. Today there are approximately fifty-five Slow Cities in Italy (including Positano), and beyond that, about twenty internationally.

ANCIENT RUINS

Positano is said to be one of the oldest settlements along the Amalfi Coast. It has traces of ancient ruins, and remains from the Palaeolithic period can be found in the grotto known as La Porta just near the main beach.

There has been an important excavation in the last decade of a large Roman villa that lies beneath the town of Positano, which was thought to have been covered by the ashes of Vesuvius during the 79 AD eruption that buried nearby Pompeii. Although its existence has been known about for many years, the actual scale and importance of this villa have only recently been appreciated as a result of some serious archaeological digging. It is now known that the site of the villa occupies the entire beachfront and goes all the way back up the mountain towards Piazza Mulini. It is being painstakingly uncovered by enthusiastic young archaeologists, who pack off unearthed artefacts to Rome for labelling and archiving.

I noticed when passing the digs under the church that some orange-coloured tubes had just been revealed. Plumbing pipes in Italy are orange, so I assumed the archaeologists had uncovered some of the church's waterworks! But on my way back up from the beach that evening I encountered a beaming archaeologist who moved aside to show me they weren't pipes at all, but the remains of a 300-year-old female skeleton. I was astonished. These finds are frequent – an ancient fresco of a horse was also unearthed a few days previously.

A SPIN AROUND TOWN

If your legs won't carry you home or you just want a *giro di paese* (spin around town), take one of the little local buses. Drivers sit poker-faced as they weave the short, refrigerator-shaped buses around precarious curves, and contend with double-parked delivery trucks, lost foreign drivers crawling along at a snail's pace, and mothers loaded with shopping and straggling ice-cream-eating toddlers. You might think you're coming to within an inch of your life, but invariably the driver manages to manoeuvre his vehicle unscathed through the obstacle course.

THE GALLI ISLANDS

The Galli Islands (below) form an archipelago just a few nautical miles from Positano, visible from almost every part of town. This group of three islands, once known as Le Sirenuse (The Sirens, said to be half bird, half woman), is one of the richest historical areas on the Amalfi Coast, and also has an important place in Greek mythology. Homer's wild and adventurous character Ulysses knew that several sirens, whose enchanting but deadly melodies lured many a passing seaman to his death, inhabited the islands. Ulysses was curious to experience these hypnotic tunes. He had his crew plug their ears with wax, strap him to the mast of his ship and sail by, so he could listen to the tunes without risking his life. He was driven to distraction listening to the sirens' sweet melodies, and begged his sailors to untie him, but they did not heed his calls (maybe it was the wax!) and he was spared. The modern name of these islands, Galli, comes from the word rooster, referring to the bird-like sirens.

Now privately owned, the islands' previous inhabitants include the Romans and the Saracens. In the early twentieth century, they became the retreat of the great Russian choreographer and dancer Leonide Massine. After his death, another world famous dancer, Rudolf Nureyev, made his home there. I spent many of my early days in Positano boating, swimming and diving around these islands. The water is especially clear and clean, and the islands form a perfect backdrop. I would often see the extravagant Nureyev jet-skiing around the islands sporting a very taut body and a very tiny tanga! When he passed away in the early '90s, the islands were purchased by a charming and stylish man I eventually met though a mutual friend, and over the years I have been lucky enough to enjoy some of the most delicious lunches and wonderful parties on these historic landmarks of the Amalfi Coast.

SHOPPING IN POSITANO

The handmade sandal is still one of the best buys in Positano. When you're wandering around the beach area you will see the tiny store **Safari**, with its eye-catching window display of plain and jewelled sandals. Take a step inside (one step is as far as you can go anyway, because that's all the room there is) and have a look around – you won't come out empty-handed.

Up the other end of the beach there are more stores that make lovely classic sandals to measure, including **Moda Positano**. Usually they will be able to make you a pair while you enjoy a day in the sun.

One of my favourite boutiques in town is the **Emporio Sirenuse**. Carla Sersale of Le Sirenuse hotel fame runs this small store right opposite the hotel. I have bought lots of Lisa Corti designs from here for gifts back home as well as for my bedroom and lounge room. Lisa Corti is a clever Milanese designer who creates wonderful fabrics and prints. She produces some of the most original work I have seen. As well as Carla's enormous variety of Lisa Corti quilts, tablecloths, pillowcases, *pareos* and dresses, she also stocks wonderful global brands such as Etro, Eres, Metradamo and Stephan Janson. The store is expensive but Carla has great sales at the end of summer, which are eagerly awaited by many shoppers.

Il Capitano is the nickname of the owner of another eccentric little shop. He acquired his name while travelling the world for much of his youth as a crew member on large ships. I am pretty sure he wasn't the captain, but this is how you acquire a nickname in Italy – by simple association. Decades ago Capitano opened his little store and he is one of the few shop-holders in Positano that stays open in the low season. In the dead of winter, long after the other shops have shut, you will often see Capitano huddled at the entrance of his shop ready for a sale.

This is the spot to purchase *ex voto* – thin, palm-sized tin icons in the shape of parts of the body. These are used as offerings to the saints when that particular part of the body is giving you grief, in an attempt to alleviate your suffering. The church of Sant' Antonino in Sorrento has the most impressive wall covered with these small icons. They are stylised and artistic, and I have covered my bathroom walls with them. I hound Capi for new ones every time I visit.

The last time I was with my mum, Maggie, in Positano we would pass by Capi's daily and have a dig around inside his dusty little shop. Aside from his usual old tiles, well-priced glasses and bronze statues we found a fabulous 50 cm × 50 cm cameo of a baby. It was so *not* Maggie, but she decided she had to have it! With a generous discount from Capi and a well-meaning guarantee regarding its 'oldness', we took it back to our apartment to pack. Adriana, my faithful shop manager for many years, told me that Capi would pop into the store every morning to say hi and to ask when Maggie and I were leaving. She only figured out after our

NICKNAMES

Sergio's dad, Adolfo, was always known as 'Pinkerton' amongst the locals because he was an avid fan of the American comic strip character of the same name. He carried this nickname for most of his life, and Sergio, being the eldest son, is still often greeted affectionately as Pinkerton. There's hardly a male *Positanese* who doesn't have a nickname, generally stemming from a prominent physical feature or personality trait, and usually the source of endless teasing. Popular nicknames were *il marchese* (the marquis – given to someone who is always well-dressed), *pirata* or *capitano* (for someone who had worked at sea), and *ciccio* (given to chubby kids, but unfortunately the nickname tends to stick, so they carry it on into old age no matter how thin they might get!)

OPPOSITE: Maria Lampo's iconic store-front mannequins from the 1960s

departure that he had been anxious to get another identical baby cameo up on the wall outside. Maggie and I laughed our heads off. You can't help loving him. I can highly recommend a stroll up the hill to Capi's store – I just can't vouch for the authenticity of every 'antique' he sells.

DIVING AROUND POSITANO

The **Centro Sub**, recently relocated to Praiano only 6 km away, is the place to go if you are interested in scuba diving. Owned and run by Gaetano Milano and Aldo Appuzzo, this dive centre has something for everyone. Aldo, Sergio and I did our NAUI (National Association of Underwater Instructors) certificates together in 1986, but while I can barely pluck up the courage for a five-metre-deep dive these days, Aldo has spent much of the last couple of decades underwater as a passionate diver and instructor.

Aldo and Gaetano have a boat for every occasion. You can dive all day and enjoy a light lunch aboard the boat between dives, or do one long morning dive followed by a leisurely meal at one of the coastal restaurants (like Ristorante il Cantuccio in Nerano). Gaetano and Aldo also offer an open-water dive certificate course for keen beginners (one hour's practical lesson and one hour's theory a day). At the end of the week-long course participants are awarded a NASE (National Academy of Scuba Educators) certificate, a step up from the PADI certification (Professional Association of Diving Instructors), which takes three days. The best dives in the area are:

- La Grotto dello Zaffiro – a nearby grotto in Nerano and close to the tiny island of Isca. The island, affectionately known as La Balena (the whale) because of its shape, possesses deep, colourful sea walls. In fact, I did my deepest dive ever off this island – 53 metres! It was pitch dark down there and we needed Hollywood-style lights to see anything. The descent was swift but I thought the ascent and its decompression would never end. Definitely a one-off for me, but I'm glad I did it.

- Ischitella – located in the nearby town of Praiano, it is home to magnificent bright red Gorgonian sea walls (a tree-like coral that grows at a depth of over 16 metres).

- Isola dei Galli – an island paradise with tropical fish (particularly parrot fish), dolphins (depending on the time of year) and turtles during summer night dives. The only thing missing are the sirens that Homer insisted ruled these waters many centuries ago.

LA CAMBUSA

SPECIALITÀ
ALLA
BRACE

PEPITO

THE BEST OF THE BEST IN POSITANO:

- Best gelato – **Buca di Bacco Bar** (but for coffee flavour, try the **Covo dei Saraceni** hotel on the beach).
- Best place to buy wine – Bar Internazionale, and the butcher downtown, **Cuomo** (surprising but true).
- Best fruit and veggies – **Ciro's** (with the yellow-and-white-striped awning). It's worth the trip up the main Amalfi Coast road to this shop that supplies most of the good restaurants and hotels.
- Best butcher – Sirocco's Macelleria, at the top of town, for good local cuts.
- Best fish shop – Pescheria Pasquale de Lucia at La Chiesa Nuova.
- Best Vietri and Solimene ceramics – **Ceramica Assunta** (opposite Le Sirenuse hotel).
- Best evening bar for drinks and people-watching – **La Pergola** (with live music) on the main beach.
- Best evening bar for drinks, music and food, with a young crowd – **Next 2**.
- Best boutique hotel – Hotel Poseidon (opposite top), for its great position and laid-back atmosphere.
- Best pasta with fish – **Bar Bruno**.
- Best fish soup – **La Cambusa**.
- Best antipasti (and the best *arancini* in the world, according to Marco) – **Taverna del Leone**.
- Best spot for a kiss – near the Madonna at A'Garritta, at the entrance of Positano, on the hill. It is also just near **Franchino's** wonderful all-night hamburger van.
- Best quiet beach for swimming, service, tranquillity and people-watching – La Scogliera, under the disco on the main beach (no kids!).
- Best busy beach for good food and atmosphere – Laurito.
- Best shoe shops – **3 Denari**, on the beach, for moccasins; Moda Positano, next door, for classic sandals; Safari for sandals with bling.
- Best linen clothing – **La Bottega di Brunella** for easy-fit, and **Pepito's** for men's shirts and fitted styles.
- Best all-round fashion buys – **Antica Sartoria**, at the main beach and in the Mulini area.
- Best bellini – Il San Pietro at sunset, made by Salvatore Bella.
- Best pizzas – La Pergola (by the slice) and **Tre Sorelle**, both in the beach area; **Saraceno d'Oro** and **Il Fornillo** restaurants in Fornillo; and Taverna del Leone in Laurito.
- Best granita – the lemon granita van in Piazza Mulini.

OPPOSITE: Producing beautiful handmade sandals inside the tiny shop at Safari (centre); Pepito and I hanging out in the doorway of his store (bottom)

61

BEACHES

During summer on the Amalfi Coast, almost every aspect of life takes place at the beach: swimming, sunbaking, talking, reading, having lunch, taking a shower, applying make-up, getting undressed, getting dressed, eating dinner, making love, singing, getting drunk, holding a concert, having a fight, taking a walk, and going to sleep.

The beach is really an extension of home – one large living room where everybody can spend time together, with everything close at hand. The Italians have made life on the beach so totally civilised that there is no point in going home – if you do, you might miss something.

A girlfriend of mine recently pointed out how much Italians love things lined up in neat rows. Nothing illustrates this better than the beaches of the Amalfi Coast at the beginning of each day in the height of summer. Every single beach is covered in perfectly neat rows of beach beds, umbrellas, boats, deckchairs and anything else that belongs by the sea. They are all arranged according to colour, shape and size, but as the day wears on, chaos takes over and the beach soon looks like a child's bedroom after a major tantrum. Because rules, as the Italians know better than anyone, are there to be broken.

La Scogliera, a small private beach at the far end of the main beach in Positano, is great for people-perving and pampering. You pay to enter at the main beach (just say 'La Scogliera *per favore*'), and the owners Cichetto and his sister Adelina will treat you to a luxurious beach experience. In the high season you have to book your beach bed in advance – this is one popular place, but terribly civilised and rarely over-crowded. You'll see everything here, from the young, glamorous jet-set to powerful businessmen accompanied by bronzed, bikini-clad girls parading in stilettos. The blue-and-white-striped beach beds and umbrellas are set up on large flat rocks (perfect for those Italian women who love to wear their heels at the beach), with just a narrow strip of volcanic pebbles for beachlovers. No kids are allowed (you'll understand why when you go) and with simple meals, wine and good coffee all served right to your beach bed, it's a pretty amazing way to spend a day.

Fornillo Beach is another favourite of mine, and boasts four beach bars – my regular hangouts are **Pupetto**, and **Da Ferdinando**, although they also serve great salads at **Grassi** and **La Marinella**. The atmosphere is relaxed, with a good mix of the young and not-so-young. You'll find locals playing cards, young tourists flirting heavily with tired but enthusiastic waiters, good music, plenty of good food, decent coffee and cold beers. It's a pleasant ten-minute walk from the main beach in Positano, or if you are up in Fornillo and planning to lunch at Pupetto, you can use the lift at Hotel Vittoria, owned by the same family. But don't try to fool them by eating elsewhere – they have a ticketing system and are vigilant about illegal lift travellers!

Another jewel of a beach restaurant is **Bagni d'Arienzo**, just three minutes by boat from Positano. Good food in a great location, with an interesting mix of locals and tourists.

PRAIANO, *IL PAESE DELL'ANTICA PLAGIANUM* (THE TOWN OF ANCIENT OPEN SEAS) POPULATION: 1900 INHABITANTS *Praianesi*
ORIGINS OF THE NAME: Its ancient name was Plagianum meaning 'open sea' DISTRICT: Vettica PATRON SAINT: San Luca Evangelista,
protector of the artist, celebrated on 18 October

MOTHER CHURCH (*CHIESA MADRE*): San Luca Evangelista **TOWERS:** Torre a Mare and Torre a Grado **TYPICAL DISH:** *Gateau di patate* (potato bake) – this dish combines the earthy, wholesome ingredients for which this region is renowned: pork salami, eggs, mozzarella and heaps of potato

'SE VUOI VIVER SANO, LA MANE A VETTICA E LA SERA A PRAIANO'

IF YOU WANT A HEALTHY LIFE, THE MORNING IN VETTICA AND THE EVENING IN PRAIANO — LOCAL SAYING

A QUIETER CORNER OF THE COAST

Praiano is the town I would live in if I ever returned to the Amalfi Coast. It is quieter, calmer, less commercial, and in many ways has been less affected by the tourist boom of the last fifty years than many other coastal towns in the area – it is still very 'local', as we say.

It might be a tranquil place, but this town has the best tourist brochure on the Amalfi Coast – it's seriously VIP! It has everything from a brief history of the town to listings of annual events and festivals, as well as every phone number you could possibly need. So your first stop should be to pick one up at the tourist information office on the main drag right next door to **Bar Sole**, my favourite bar in Praiano. Bar Sole serves a great cappuccino and is *the* meeting point in town, a bit like Bar Internazionale is in Positano. Don't expect any special treatment; the visitors just blend in with the local trade in these spots. If the tourist office is closed – as it will be during the long siesta after lunch – and you need some information, just try asking at the bar; they can tell you just about anything you need to know.

Praiano has always been known for its rich soil and sunny position on the coast, which enables the cultivation of excellent vegetables, especially potatoes and oranges, which are the very best in the region. Three oranges are depicted on the communal crest of the town. I go here to eat and to relax, if not in a restaurant, then at a friend's home – everyone in Praiano knows how to throw together a great meal! My dear friend Giovanni Scala, a local historian who has published many books on the town, has fed me many times during my years living on the coast. Giovanni has a pizza oven in a large room tucked under his house, and knows plenty about pizza-making. His entire family is musical and each member can either sing like an angel or play some unique and wonderful instrument. A night at Giovanni's was always a great treat, singing Neapolitan songs, strumming any instrument at hand and eating stacks of pizza. One night Sergio ate more than five pizzas, singing the entire time. I could not believe my eyes!

PROTECTING THE PRAIANESI

In centuries past Praiano was chiefly a fishing village, some say way before Cetara became the iconic fishing town of the area. But the *Praianesi* have always been a prosperous people, producing beautiful silks and linens, working busy paper mills and supplying the Maritime Republic of Amalfi with chestnut, beech and poplar wood for boatbuilding. In 1924 a monster flood destroyed the town's main sea access, forcing the locals to move up the mountain, and they continue to work both the mountains and the sea to this day.

The marvellous defence towers of Praiano, Torre a Mare (left) and Torre a Grado, like many others along the coastline, were built during the Middle Ages. The structures are called Saracen towers, named after the intruders they were built to ward off. The Saracens would arrive by boat, ransack villages, rape and kidnap women and steal all the locals' worldly goods. The smoke from fires lit in the towers was a very effective warning system to the next town of imminent danger, giving the townsfolk time to hide their women, children and treasures up in the hills. The invaders often left empty-handed.

FAMILY-STYLE CELEBRATIONS

When the *Praianesi* celebrate anything, they do it as a family. La Notte in Bianco (the sleepless night) is an all-night feast celebrated in August, and it's a full-on family affair. The whole town stays up all night; even the butcher makes his presence known, selling meat till 3 a.m. You can buy a nail at the hardware store till 4 a.m., and the best local deli, **Tutto per Tutti**, will offer you a glass of wine when you wander in at midnight to buy some eggs. Recently, La Notte in Bianco kicked off with the newly established five-star hotel, **Casa Angelina**, offering a generous buffet to the locals. The festivities usually continue until well after sunrise and wind up sometime around 9 a.m. The *Praianesi* know how to party!

The locals love to eat and drink together *al aperto* (in the open). Another longstanding event occurs on the day of San Martino, 11 November, when the *Praianesi* celebrate the first drops of wine made from that year's harvest and share what they have produced. (If you stay in a small family-run *pensione* anywhere on the Amalfi Coast, you will sometimes get to try their homemade wine and you'll often be pleasantly surprised.) Large tables of wine and food are set up in the piazza of San Luca and the whole town gathers to celebrate.

Every Friday night from the end of July through August, you can enjoy the Festival of Traditions, where Neapolitan music and dance are performed as well as traditional music from many parts of the world.

THE GUITAR-MAKERS OF PRAIANO

Pasquale Scala (left, Giovanni's brother) makes the most beautiful guitars and mandolins. He is known throughout Italy for his mastery as a *liutaio* (maker of stringed instruments). Pasquale's young son Leonardo has followed in his father's footsteps, working as an *intarsiatore* (inlayer), adding intricate decorations to the instruments in mother-of-pearl, shell, lambskin or bone. Pasquale's speciality is the antique mandolin, which has distinct Arabic influences. Pasquale and Leonardo make beautiful replicas of these ancient instruments as well as modern-day classical guitars, taking up to three months to complete each unique piece.

When my son Marco was a schoolboy he learnt the guitar for three years. My dream was that he would continue into his teens so I could ask Pasquale to make a special guitar for him one day. But it was not to be. Unless Pasquale has taken up soccer-ball production, we won't be able to do business.

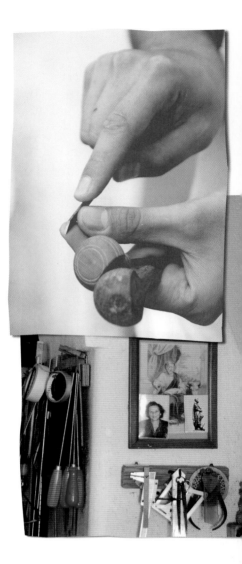

FESTIVAL OF FLAMES

One of the prettiest celebrations on the coast, the Festival of San Domenico, has been going for over 400 years. Legend has it that before giving birth to San Domenico, his mother dreamt of a dog with a flaming torch in its mouth. This was interpreted to mean that her son should spend his life spreading the word of God. From 1–4 August, every balcony, terrace and piazza is brightly lit with tiny candles for the celebration, but most beautiful of all is the piazza in front of the church of San Gennaro. Already a wonderful mosaic of coloured tiles by day, at night it is illuminated with 3000 tiny candles. San Domenico is an important saint in this town; a beautiful monastery in his name is attached to the church of Santa Maria delle Grazie a Castro and can be visited on the famous **Walk of the Gods**.

WALK OF THE GODS

There are an abundance of interesting walks to do around the Amalfi Coast. One of the most popular walks in this area is called the Walk of the Gods, and it follows an undulating path that was originally used by the Romans during the 4th century AD to transport goods around the mountains. The final leg of the five–six hour walk begins in Praiano and travels across the top ridge of the Lattari Mountains to Nocelle, just above Positano. It's best attempted with an accredited guide – I can recommend **Frank Carpegna** or **Maurizio de Rosa**, who each run walking tours in the area. The last time I visited Praiano I caught up with Frank, who is an old friend, and we did this walk together. It takes about three to four hours, depending on how energetic you are feeling and, as with most physical activity in Italy, there is a reward of food at the end! The walk winds up at Nocelle, where you can enjoy a delicious lunch at Santa Croce restaurant, which has some of the most spectacular views on the coast.

TOP: The elegant and capable hands of Leonardo Scala

MIDDLE: Some of the unique tools used to make stringed instruments

BOTTOM AND OVERLEAF: Sights from the Walk of the Gods

The walk takes in the magnificent monastery of San Domenico, which is perched beautifully on the hillside, affording panoramic views of the coastline. The monastery was built in the fifteenth century AD. It was recently inhabited by a group of Colombian monks for a period until 2004, but now stands empty. Although the monastery is quite run-down today, as you wander through the open space of the church you will be amazed at the brilliant and incredibly well-kept frescos that adorn the walls.

After a hearty lunch and well-deserved rest, Frank then takes you down the 2000 steps that lead back to the main road – it will leave your calf muscles aching for days!

ART

The residents of Praiano have always loved their arts and the town was recently adopted by one of America's finer contemporary minimalist artists, Sol LeWitt, who lived here part-time. A donation of one of his works to the local council has cemented their interest in developing the arts in this area. A progressive project called PRAIART is underway to develop social and cultural meeting areas, a sculpture garden and a foundation for LeWitt, who passed away in 2007.

A good friend of mine and Praiano resident is the well-established artist **Paolo Sandulli**. Paolo has frequent exhibitions on the Amalfi Coast, including in serious cultural centres such as Ravello. I love all his work, including his sculpture, painting and sketches. His women are sexy and round and full of life, whether floating under water with sea monsters or whacking a tennis ball over the net in teeny weeny miniskirts! His sculptures are full of fantasy and humour. You can find his work everywhere on the Amalfi Coast; in hotels, restaurants and private villas, and if you are dining at Positano's Hotel Palazzo Murat, scattered through their Eden-like garden you will see his distinctive smiling-face vases sporting luscious plants for hair (or you might see his new sculptures, which are crowned with enormous sea sponges). They are all delightful. Most of all I love to visit Paolo in his studio, in the Torre a Mare, right on the water, where he creates his masterpieces. Paolo's studio is open to the public and this is truly a worthwhile visit.

SHOPPING IN PRAIANO

If you are looking for something fun for the kitchen, a good buy in this town can be found at **Ceramica Liz Art**. All their merchandise is created and fired on the premises by Ventura and his brother Alfonso. And if you're wondering why there are lemons painted onto so many plates, vases and tiles, it is because the boys' father and grandfather were leading lemon traders back in the day when the Amalfi Coast produced more than 8 per cent of Italy's lemons.

I found the location for my little store in Positano all those years ago through my good friend Marcelo, a local jewellery designer originally from Argentina.

Frank Carpegna is an American with roots in Italy who I first met twenty years ago when he and his wife came to Positano for a holiday. Sergio and I became good friends with them, and after many years visiting Positano, Frank decided to move there permanently. Passionate about the outdoors, Frank qualified as a guide and set up his own walking tours company over a decade ago. His knowledge of the history and geography of the area is second-to-none, and his walks are always lots of fun, accompanied as they are by his infectious enthusiasm and delightful singing voice!

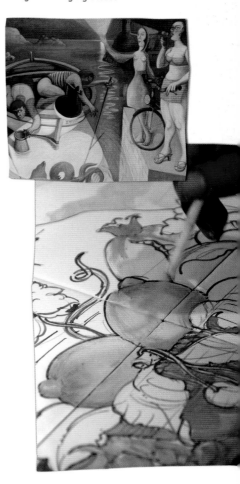

OPPOSITE: Artist Paolo Sandulli tucked away in his studio with some of his latest sculptures and watercolour sketches of local *Praianesi*

ABOVE: Skilful hands at Ceramica Liz Art demonstrating the delicate art of painting ceramics

HEALING WITH THE MAGIC TOUCH
Pasquale Aiello is a master of eastern martial arts and was Marco's Aikido instructor. He is also a master healer for any serious aches or pains. Pasquale's daughter Marina gives a wonderful massage. Like her dad, she has the magic touch – and better still, she will come to you.

ABOVE: The contemporary interior of the popular Casa Angelina

BELOW: Colour-coordinated sunbeds at the poolside of the Tramonto D'Oro hotel

OPPOSITE: The pool at Tramonto D'Oro at sunset, looking back towards Capri

He had a tiny boutique in Positano, and when the barber next door was shutting up shop, he called me immediately. Marcelo made wonderful jewellery; in fact, all the money I made in my shop I would spend in his next door! When Marcelo headed back to Argentina, I was distraught. No one could make beautiful earrings and rings like Marcelo could. But a year or two later, I discovered Renato and his chic little shop **Re Jewels** in Praiano. Over the years Renato has made some wonderful pieces for my family and me. Most of all I love the moonstone ring he made for my mother, Maggie, and the wonderful stone he set for my sister-in-law, Nicole. He has also strung some fantastic pearls for the queen of pearls, my friend Sandra Belcredi. He has a very personal contemporary style but will set to suit the client and does wonderful remodelling of existing jewellery.

A PERFECT NIGHT OUT IN PRAIANO

My gorgeous friend Sandra, or as I call her, Sandrina, first took me for a drink at Casa Angelina when it opened a few years ago. A local resident since childhood, Sandra is an expert on the best places to go in Praiano for good food, fun and ambience (and she is one of the chicest people I know, next to my mother). She is well known for her bare feet and her incredible colour sense, often wearing fluid purple or emerald silks, always accompanied by a gigantic ruby or a strand of pearls wrapped around her ankle, neck or wrist.

A favourite haunt of Sandrina's, Casa Angelina is a young and contemporary hotel with an old-fashioned name. This is the hot spot for an evening drink at sunset. It hangs right over the sea at the entrance of town as you arrive from Positano. This precious little hotel pays no homage to tradition; against a stark white background, multi-coloured Venetian glass statues from Murano jump out in a refreshing display of colour. An almost vertical driveway takes you down to the front door, and if you are nervous about getting back up this hairpin drive on your motorbike, like I was, a charming staff member will give you a lift in the hotel golf buggy while a colleague drives your Vespa up to the road (how embarrassing!).

My favourite restaurant in Praiano is a Slow Food gem. **La Brace** has been run by Gianni for over twenty-five years, and it is here that I enjoyed many romantic dinners with Sergio in our early years together. Although some tourists do come here, it is very much a local eatery. Fried prawns in their shells, local fish baked in a hard shell of salt, sautéed local broad beans and Gianni's simple tomato-based spaghetti are all a must to try at La Brace. You won't be disappointed. Don't forget to book – Gianni is always busy.

For a late-night cocktail Sandrina and I would often go to **La Fioriere**. Luigi runs this cute little hotel on the main road, almost next door to La Brace, with the friendliest service around. It is busy after dinner, perfect for a nightcap, and is often open till late.

La Brace is right opposite the **Tramonto D'Oro** (Golden Sunset), a great four-star hotel with a fabulous roof-top pool. Not only are the views spectacular, but you can catch the last rays of the day here, just as its name suggests.

DIVING OFF PRAIANO

Years ago, after Sergio and I had learnt to scuba dive, we would sneak up the coast to Praiano for a quick dive when Da Adolfo's was quiet. This area is famous for its red Gorgonian sea walls, just off the rocks near the **Tritone Hotel**. The hotel has great beach access and is a perfect spot to catch the sun. Sergio's brother Daniele would drive us up on his boat and drop us directly into the water with our tanks and gear, and then come back to fetch us an hour or so later.

One particular day, we came up early because Sergio was tired – he seemed almost too tired to even reach the nearby shore. We dog-paddled slowly to the rocky shore. Sergio was twice my weight and the thought of him needing my assistance in the water was terrifying. When we eventually arrived at the bathing area of the hotel, I left Sergio recovering by the water while I scrambled up onto the rocks and flapped towards the beach bar – tank, hot-pink flippers, mask and all – to call Daniele to come and pick us up in a hurry. The clients sunning themselves outside this luxury hotel were gobsmacked by the sight of a frazzled and teary diver emerging from the sea. The staff was very obliging and naturally Sergio, built like a bullock, was absolutely fine. I swore never to go diving again unless the boat stuck around.

EATING AND DRINKING

A few curves along the coast towards Amalfi and down by the sea is La Praia, a busy beach area that is also home to the famous disco **Africana**, just a walk around the rocks. This is the area where the floods hit in 1924, but today it is back to fishing, eating and dancing.

I have spent many a late night at Africana, a renowned nightclub from the 1950s and '60s, when people like Jackie Kennedy Onassis were frequent guests. It is housed in an enormous cave cut into the side of the mountain at sea level, with transparent glass panels built into the dance floor so you can watch the fish swim below. Small, naturally formed blowholes are tucked away in various corners around the nightclub – it's fascinating. In my early days in Positano we would arrive by sea or by land, and the charming and ever-present owner Luca kept the dance floor rocking till the wee hours. As a treat for hungry revellers, he would drop enormous fishing nets into the sea to collect whatever was passing by, and it would then be mercilessly fried up and handed around the dance floor.

Luca also managed to convince some of the sexy female dancers from the Lido in Paris to come to Praiano for their summer holidays. He fed them and found

ON THE BEACH

When I am having a 'hang out in Praiano' day with Sandrina, we often head down to **One Fire**, the coolest little beach bar, which serves a great *panino* and plays fabulous music. When people are overheating but don't feel like climbing down the ladder into the sea, one of the owners will come around with an ice-cold spray pump attached to his back, like he's applying garden fertiliser, and spray down the customers! It is crazy and delicious. This is not your conventional beach bar but it's the best fun.

And if we feel like a pasta-and-wine lunch, we go next door to **La Gavitella**, which offers a fabulous seafood menu (they also own a local fish market up the coast) and a good boat service back to Positano. These two beach establishments share the same rock but attract quite a different clientele.

them free board in local houses in return for a whirl around the disco at midnight. Beautiful bare bottoms, bosoms, stilettos and feathers would entertain us during peak season at Africana – clever Luca! Although he is no longer with us, the disco is still there and is well worth a drink and a dance after dinner.

Just two rocky curves along from Africana is another favourite spot of mine for dinner or lunch, **Il Pirata**. A candlelit dinner here is incredibly romantic, right on the water with the twinkling lights of the coastline and the tinkling of the nearby fishing boats. Il Pirata produce spectacular 'seafood anything' – baked, fried, grilled, atop pasta or in a risotto, they really have mastered the fruits of the sea. I also love the wonderful Pino Daniele music they play there – he's today's best modern Neapolitan guitarist and singer.

The well-known restaurant **Da Armandino** is also a great spot for lunch or dinner right on the beach at La Praia among the fishing boats. Armando does a delicious antipasto, a great seafood platter and light, easy pasta dishes. Keep your eyes on the ground though – it's alive with felines waiting for a little fishy treat.

Next door, **Bar Mare** is *the* spot for great music, ambience and a good snack. Sandrina and I have often arrived here very late at night after a Ravello concert and Salvatore, the son of the owner, Clelia, would always find us something from the kitchen, even jumping in there himself and whipping up a pasta if his mum had gone home for the night. But Clelia is the foundation of this little restaurant, and from a large family of fisherfolk, she is one of the few women on this coast that can handle the sea and all its treasures. Everyone is treated like family in this place.

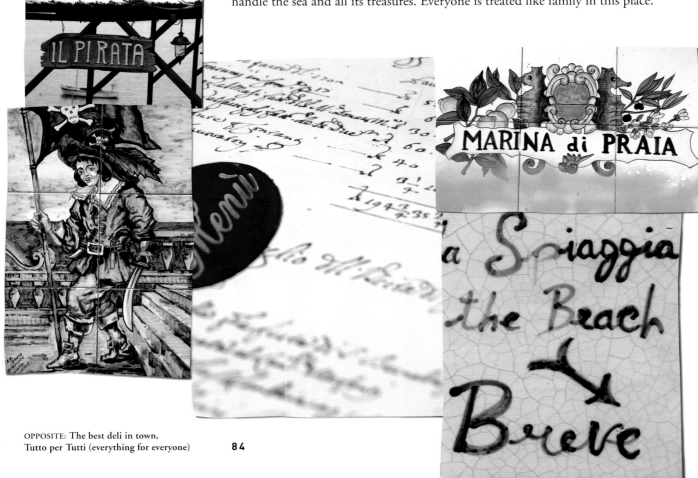

BOYS

'Don't let him cry too hard or too long, or you'll give him a hernia!' This is what the locals would say to me when Marco was a baby. You don't let boys cry in this part of the world. While his sister does the ironing, washes the dishes, tends to the garden and does the shopping, little Luigi is free to sit around and be pampered. And as for finding a wife to please him? He will never find anyone as good as Mamma.

That said, the reputation of the laid-back Neapolitan who supposedly works as little as possible does not apply to the boys of the Amalfi Coast. They are anything but lazy. Seasonal work is a killer, as I found out over the years I lived there. These guys have to pack it all in to a short period of time – they have to make money, have fun, catch up with visiting mates, find love, dance into the night and get up super early to do it all over again the next day. They work hard and play even harder, and they do it seven days a week for at least six months of the year. But it can't be doing them any harm – they all look terrific!

Of all the summer jobs, I think the boat boy's work is the hardest, spending long hours under the boiling hot summer sun. When I first met Sergio, he was a boat boy and also worked on the grill at the restaurant. He would be on the boat all morning ferrying customers to the restaurant from Positano, then when the boat service finished at lunchtime he would bolt up the stairs and cook fish for three hours on the open-air grill, which was as hot as a pizza oven. Then at 4 p.m., he would be back on the boat doing it all again till 7 or 8 p.m. A long, hot, exhausting day.

'ATTACHED TO ONE OF THE WALLS ALMOST SUSPENDED MID-AIR, A FEW LEAN FISHERMEN'S HOUSES HAVE RISEN. A GENTLE AND SOFT LIGHT DESCENDS FROM THE SKY AND RISES FROM THE SEA… AT THE ENTRANCE OF THE FIORD OF FURORE.'

RICCARDO BACCHELLI, WELL-KNOWN ITALIAN WRITER

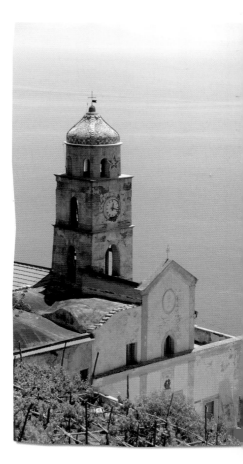

THE TOWN THAT DEFIES GRAVITY

Furore clings to the sides of the Lattari Mountains that embrace the entire Amalfi Coast, and then descends dramatically to the sea. It gives the impression of being shy, almost hiding itself away from the sometimes overcrowded coastline. Furore 'floats' between the sea and the mountains like a passing cloud, and the small coloured houses of the town appear suspended in the sky.

Il paese che non c'e (the town that is not there) or *il paese dipinto* (the town of paintings) are the descriptions you read on signs as you arrive in Furore. This is how Furore has been known since Raffaele Ferraioli (the ever-present mayor) established this town's identity. And although Furore does not boast the classic cluster of Moorish roofs huddled around a delightful piazza with a church in the middle, like so many other coastal towns, it does have some wonderful sites that are testimony to its remarkable identity.

OPPOSITE: The magnificent fiord of Furore, with the *monazzeni* (fishermen's houses) nestled into the side of the mountain

ABOVE: The quaint hilltop church of San Giaccomo

95

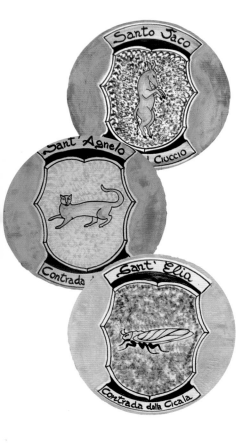

There is an upper and a lower part to this pretty hanging village. The lower part is easily visited as one drives along the snake-like coastal road, admiring the rich blues of the Mediterranean waters beneath. The upper part can be accessed by a road that curls up the mountain through richly perfumed lemon groves and vineyards. And because of this extraordinary geography, the locals enjoy a wonderful mix of both sea and land gastronomy.

The vertiginous village of Furore is divided into three districts, named after the individual parish symbols. Il Ciuccio (the donkey) is the symbol for the parish of San Giaccomo Apostolo. For the Greeks and Romans the donkey represented fertility. La Gatta (the cat), renowned for surviving under difficult conditions, belongs to San Michele Arcangelo and represents liberty and femininity. La Cicala (the cicada) is attached to the parish of Sant' Elia and is the symbol of immortality, spirituality and life after death.

THE FIORD

Perhaps the most remarkable thing about Furore is its magnificent fiord. This spectacular 'wound on the coast' slices through the land from the very top of the mountains in Agerola all the way down to the sea. The water is swimming-pool calm in the summer months and monstrously turbulent during the winter. It is delightful to visit in summer in a small boat; it's like entering an open-air cave (but watch out for swimmers). For the last twenty years or so, at the beginning of July, Furore has hosted a High Diving Championship called The Mediterranean Cup. The dive takes place on the Amalfi Coast road from the bridge that traverses the famous fiord. Brave young souls from all over the world swan-dive 28 metres off the bridge into the fiord. The winners are usually Colombians or Americans (though in 2005 the Australian, Joe Zuber, took the cup home). This is an awesome event not to be missed.

It is also charming to wander down the steps featured in the Roberto Rossellini film, *L'Amore*, starring Anna Magnani (the couple famously took up residency in one of the characteristic fishermen's houses nestled into the side of the fiord while filming). The steps run from the main road and lead to a small museum, restaurant and beach. The museum houses everyday artefacts dating back centuries, including walking sticks, cigar boxes, knives, combs and buttons, all carved from horn – a special art that was practised in this area until the 1950s.

If you take the steps down to the beach, just below Rossellini's old house, you'll find **Al Monazeno**, a tiny beachside trattoria. Luigi runs the show and, like many restaurant owners on the coast, he speaks better English than I do! A recent day out with my journalist mate Michele brought us to this wonderful spot. Luigi served us a delicious swordfish, rocket and *piennolo* tomato pasta. Topped off with a cooling dip in the fiord, it was a perfect day in unforgettable surroundings.

OPPOSITE: The only other way down to the fiord (if you're not diving) is this delightful staircase where many scenes of *L'Amore* were filmed

IL PAESE DIPINTO

Artists love *il paese dipinto*, and Furore loves its artists. The town has embraced well-known European artists such as German Fritz Gilow, Polish Werner Christian Wontroba, Franco-Argentinean Marco Lopez Bernal and numerous renowned Italian artists. Walking around Furore is like a visit to an open-air contemporary art gallery. The walls of many public and private buildings are covered with large, sometimes loud paintings. This unusual initiative to encourage artistic expression was put in place over twenty years ago and has given this scenic town an individual identity. Each hairpin curve reveals a creative painting on a wall or a sculpture nestled into a small street garden. Every year Furore invites a dozen artists from all over the world to execute their works of art on the walls of the town. I asked Raffaele Ferraioli what will happen when they run out of walls, but he assures me they have plenty left.

Lovers of classic culture shouldn't miss the fifteenth-century triptych (below) by Angelo Antonello de Capua in the precious little church of Sant' Elia. This beautiful work is one of the most important pieces of art on the Amalfi Coast. And the exquisite fresco by Neapolitan Roberto di Odorisio, of the Giotto school, can be seen in the church crypt of San Giaccomo.

costiera dei fiori

EATING AND DRINKING

Furore has a special significance for me. Sergio took me there years ago for a wonderful night at **Bacco Hotel and Restaurant**. We eagerly drove up the mountain one chilly winter's night and enjoyed a delicious meal of traditional dishes: tasty local eggplant, creamy mozzarella, light homemade pasta and juicy baked pork, accompanied by excellent local wines.

On a more recent visit to Bacco, I followed a delicious lunch with some great local cheeses from nearby Tramonti. They served two different types: *caciocavallo* cheese (which Marco grew up on), one matured and one fresh; and sheep's cheese, again one matured and one fresh. All the cheeses were served with local honey, homemade sweet green tomato chutney and local *freselle*, a rock-hard dried wholemeal bread that is softened very quickly in water just before eating. What a gastronomic treat!

Freselle is also the basic ingredient for the famous *insalata caponata* of this area. In Positano we would make *caponata* with *freselle*, *piennolo* tomatoes, rocket and mozzarella to take on our boat trips. But in Furore they use eggplant and anchovies in place of the rocket and mozzarella, and in Cetara they use tuna in place of mozzarella. All the towns on the Amalfi Coast seem to have their own interpretation of this dish.

On a boat trip years ago with some friends from this area, we forgot to bring fresh water on board and only had wine – typical! Naturally this *caponata* salad is prepared just before eating, so we drifted our boat very close to a grotto and dipped the *freselle* very quickly in the crystal clear water. We didn't need to add salt; the sea had done it for us. It was incredibly good.

MUST-TRIES IN FURORE

- *Pomodorini a piennolo*: These perfect small tomatoes are dried in bunches around this town and give off a perfume of rich earth and salty sea. They are available from the end of summer onwards and are best prepared as a simple pasta sauce with garlic and olive oil.

- Baby new potatoes: These are particularly good in this area, so try them if you can. Make sure they are from Furore.

- *L'uva pizzutella* (grapes) preserved under aniseed: These are spectacular. You will also find figs and apricots treated the same way – they are equally delicious.

HIKING

The best lookout from this amazing town is right above it on the edge of the dairy-producing village of Agerola (if you need milk or cheese, grab it here.) It is called *Punta Corona* and will take your breath away. And in town, ask around for the good walking tracks – there are plenty.

FIVE-STAR ACCOMMODATION

For amazing views and multiple-swimming pool, five-star accommodation, visit the Furore Inn Resort (pictured opposite, top left).

LEFT: The classic Neapolitan Pulcinella eating up a storm at Bacco restaurant

The amazing wine we drank at Bacco was made across the road at **Marisa Cuomo Wines**, run by Marisa and her husband Andrea Ferraioli, who together took over the family business that had been in Andrea's family for generations.

Marisa and Andrea produce some of the best wines on the Amalfi Coast. Fiorduva is their latest hero and ranks as one of the great Vini Estremi (Extreme Wines) of this country. The robust grapes that produce these wines are grown under the most challenging conditions. Situated 500 metres above sea level, seemingly hanging in space like the rest of the town, their vineyards are subject to difficult climatic conditions, and the terrain is exhausting for the growers. Italy is renowned for its Vini Estremi: from the great wines of Etna, Trentino-Alto Adige, Sardinia, Valle d'Aosta, the island of Pantelleria and the Amalfi Coast, all these areas of geographic extremes produce excellent wines. The Fiorduva has won numerous national and international awards over the last ten years, including the prestigious Tre Bicchieri (Three Glasses) award, given by the *Gambero Rosso Guide*. Marisa's reserve reds have also won many recent awards and are worth trying.

Winemaking has a long history in this region. The Italian wine first drunk by the Romans in Tiberius's time came from Campania. This area still produces a great variety of wine grapes and there are some great wineries to visit in the region. Gaetano Marrone, my wine guru friend, has an immense knowledge of local and regional wines. As well as being the Vice Mayor of Positano and the representative of the Slow Food Association on the Amalfi Coast, he is also sommelier at Le Terrazze restaurant on the main beach of Positano. Here are some of his suggestions for local wines to try, ranging from the most expensive to the cheapest:

REDS

Montevetrano (producer: Montevetrano, Salerno). Full bodied and silky.

Taurasi Riserva (producer: Mastrobernardino, Irpinia). Earthy flavours.

Aglianico d'Irpina (producer: I Favati, Irpinia). Dry, with highlights of pepper and liquorice.

WHITES

Fiorduva (producer: Marisa Cuomo Wines, Furore). Dry and exotic.

Greco G. (producer: Pietracupa, Irpinia). Dry with citrus highlights.

Fiano di Avellino (producer: Villa Diamante, Irpinia). Dry with mineral highlights.

OPPOSITE: The queen of vino on the Amalfi Coast, Marisa Cuomo

THE VILLA OF VATS

From the Amalfi Coast road, just before you reach the Furore bridge that straddles the fiord, you will see a large abstract-looking villa built into the rock. On closer inspection, you'll see it is made up of *botte* (large wine vats). The story goes that just after the war the owner did not want to declare taxable building materials, so he cleverly placed one enormous vat on top of another, until he had created his paradise.

STAIRS & STONES

These are two things you can't miss on the Amalfi Coast - they're everywhere!

When I first moved here, the one thing I had to get used to was *facendo le scale* (doing the stairs). It didn't matter where I was going or whom I was visiting, stairs were just part of getting there.

Taking the stairs will always cut off a few curves (your's and the road's) and get you where you want to go faster, but they can be exhausting. Watch the locals; the trick is to do them s-l-o-w-l-y, for the sake of your knees and your lungs, especially in hot weather. You will often see locals having a chat on the stairs rather than in the street or the piazza – it's a good excuse to have a rest.

The worst stairs are known as 'donkey stairs' – stairs that are so low and deep that you end up having to use the same leg to step up each stair. They are so-called because they are in those parts of town that are inaccessible by car or truck, so donkeys are still used to cart materials up and down.

If you come from a part of the world blessed with wide sandy beaches, the thought of lying on a pebbled beach will not be the most comfortable prospect. But you do get used to it. And once you get used to it, you'll find you can't stand the sticky sand.

Adolfo always swore by the health benefits of these small volcanic pebbles. He would lie flat on his back on the stones on the beach, claiming they helped ease numerous ailments, from poor digestion to arthritis and aching legs. I remember on the days when his arthritis was really bad, he would rush down to the beach and lie on the hot black stones until his body was covered in small red craters and welts.

The playful side of Adolfo saw another use for these stones. He would sit quietly on the beach, whistling to himself and looking around unassumingly. He would then scoop up a handful of small pebbles and shoot them like a rifle straight at your anklebones – it hurt like hell! He would always laugh himself silly afterwards.

One of my earliest impressions of the pebbled beaches was how wonderful they looked in winter, especially after rough seas. The reason for this was that when building renovations resumed at the end of summer, all the vivid coloured ceramic tiles from ripped-up floors and walls used to be thrown down into the sea. Over time, these small bits of broken terracotta would become rounded, retaining a splash of colour in the middle, and would wash up on the shore after a big swell. I would lug up bags of these ceramic pebbles from the beach every day and eventually I made a mosaic coffee-table from them. Today you can still see ceramic pebbles wedged into walls and terraces of private villas, but you will rarely see them washed up on the shores, as discarded building materials are no longer dumped at sea.

di Padova, protector of lost objects, the hungry and the poor, celebrated on 13 June MOTHER CHURCH (*CHIESA MADRE*): San Pacrazio Martire TOWER: Capo di Conca TYPICAL DISH: Officially, *la sfogliatella* (sweet pastries), but a lesser-known delicacy is rabbit baked in lemon leaves; if you are staying for a while, beg one of the locals to make it for you – it is delicious.

'IN OGNI FINESTRA IL SOLE, DA OGNI FINESTRA IL MARE'

IN EVERY WINDOW THE SUN, FROM EVERY WINDOW THE SEA — LOCAL SAYING

FALLING FOR CONCA

My sister-in-law Nicole and I often talked about taking a house in Conca dei Marini, known as Conca. 'The ideal weekender,' we would say. Quiet, with plenty of mountain air and sea views, each little whitewashed house has its own four walls and plenty of space between you and the next-door neighbour. The town is small but feels spacious and every property appears to possess a wonderful lemon orchard, so the entire town is perfumed with lemon! Even while living only ten kilometres away in Positano, we thought this easy little town could offer us some tranquillity and sanity on weekends. Of course, this was a total fantasy – the busiest time of the week for us was the weekend in Positano. But we could still dream . . .

I love Conca. The people are extremely friendly – especially the cheeky local kids, who are great fun. You get invited to eat at a local *Conchesi's* kitchen table whenever there is a meal being prepared, even if they hardly know you. And practically everyone's name is Antonio (after their patron saint), so you can hardly go wrong. The last time I was there for the saint's day on 13 June, I ran into three ex-staff members of Da Adolfo's – all called Antonio!

The first time I ever visited Conca was when Marco, then about nine years old, persuaded me to take him to kayaking lessons twice a week with his school friends for the entire summer holiday. I would pop Marco on the back of my Vespa and drive him to Conca for lessons. The course was not in the pretty little protected area of Marina di Conca, but in the fully exposed area of the Lido di Conca, just under the sixteenth-century tower, Capo di Conca. This place was fiercely windy and these little kids would paddle like mad and not move at all. It was exhausting for them and exhausting for us anxious mothers watching from the shore. But they loved it and would always come back laughing and full of seafaring advice. The instructor was passionate and worked the kids into a frenzy.

One day I took all six kids out to Conca on the boat from Positano. It was a particularly windy day and after several attempts to dock at the jetty I finally

CONCA

WHERE TO FIND *SFOGLIATELLA*
Although there is no longer a *sfogliatella* festival in Conca, you will often find this traditional and delicious pastry at other summer celebrations. You'll also find them up and down the coast in good pastry shops such as Bar Gambardella in Minori or Pasticceria Pansa in Amalfi.

managed to disembark everyone. I decided to stay on the boat as it was very gusty and there were no buoys available, just the anchor. I dropped anchor close by to wait for them to finish their lesson. But I fell asleep in the sun and woke up twenty minutes later in a totally different spot! The wind had dragged my anchor and the boat had drifted – out to sea, thank goodness, and not onto the rocks. Sergio would have skinned me; I was driving his precious forty-year-old *gozzo*. We stuck to the motorbike from then on.

THE *SFOGLIATELLA* OF SANTA ROSA

Conca is famous for its *sfogliatella di Santa Rosa*, a light pastry created some time in the early 1700s in the kitchens of the convent of Santa Rosa by the resident nuns. It is a light, layered pastry stuffed with sweet rich ricotta and topped with a cherry. Today, this *dolce* is known not only all over Italy, but in many parts of the world. In the 1800s renowned Neapolitan pastry chef Pasquale Pintauro somehow got his hands on the Santa Rosa recipe. He modified it a bit here and a bit there and called it a typical Neapolitan *dolce*, a claim still made today. But the *Conchesi* know the truth.

The Santa Rosa convent (left) is an impressive piece of architecture. It seems to hang suspended in space over the bright Mediterranean waters at the entrance of the town and dates back to the mid-1500s, when it was given to Conca by the Archbishop of Amalfi, Giovanni Ferdinando Annio. Over a hundred years later it was passed on to Sister Maria Pandolfo, who oversaw the Dominican order in this convent. A decade or so later the nuns were busy in the kitchens of the convent inventing the wonderful *sfogliatella*. They would distribute this treat among the townsfolk every year on 30 August, the day of Santa Rosa. The convent is being restored by its new owner and may soon be converted into a glamorous hotel.

SANT'ANTONIO

The evening of 13 June, the festival of Sant' Antonio di Padova, is a great night to visit Conca. Sant' Antonio's large and impressive figure is brought out of the mother church and walked around the village in a wonderful procession involving the entire town (right). The band is always a well-known one from the region. The recent procession I attended was led by the Gran Concerto Bandistico Citta' di Fisciano, consisting of forty enthusiastic musicians, many wearing one earring and all sporting dark 'Blues Brothers' sunglasses in the evening light. I was fascinated to discover most of them had their own weekend rock band and these religious festivals were just part of everyday life for these aspiring young musicians.

SAN PANCRAZIO

My favourite church in this town is San Pancrazio (left). Sergio's cousin from Cetara married here years ago and I remember vividly making our way up the narrow hairpin bends to this wonderfully delicate church, which is surrounded by exotic palms. It is a picture-perfect, advent-calendar-type church. The church also houses many fascinating *ex voto* that belonged to courageous sailors who survived brutal seas and storms.

CAPO DI CONCA TOWER

One of the grandest and better conserved towers on the Amalfi Coast is Capo di Conca (bottom left). Majestically protruding into the Mediterranean, it sits further out than any coastal tower. In centuries past, this tower controlled the entire signals activity up and down the coast; it had a bird's-eye view to the east towards Amalfi and Salerno, and to the west towards Positano and Capri. Today it is one of the few towers that is not privately owned. It is run by the local council and exhibits marine artefacts as well as being used for occasional exhibitions.

THE GROTTA DELLO SMERALDO

The stunning Grotta dello Smeraldo (right) in Conca is considered by many to be the eighth natural wonder of the world. In my opinion it is as beautiful, if not more beautiful, than the more well-known Grotto Azzurro of Capri. It was discovered by a local fisherman over seventy years ago, although the Hotel Luna in Amalfi has documentation that goes back to the mid-1800s encouraging 'enthusiastic travellers to view this newly discovered phenomenon in the neighbouring town of Conca'. The inside of this grotto is crowded with stalactites and stalagmites up to ten metres tall and contains the brightest emerald-green water, which is lit by the light that passes under the rocky walls of the cave.

But the most fabulous thing about this grotto for me is the guides who row you around in the boats. Visitors are divided between flat-bottomed boats; there is the German boat, the English boat, the French boat, and so on. Naturally, the guides speak all languages. The problem is that everything they say sounds Neapolitan. You can listen to a charming account of the caves in Neapo-English, Neapo-German or Neapo-French. The spiel is not really important; the visual beauty of this grotto says it all, but the guides are entertaining!

WEDDINGS, PARTIES, ANYTHING
An early trip to Conca led me to discover the best videographer, who shot all my fashion shows, **Sabatino Laudano.** I have since discovered that he is also your man for wedding videos.

MARINA DI CONCA

Down on the tiny beach of Marina di Conca, recognised as one of the ten most beautiful beaches in Italy, nestles one of the prettiest chapels I have ever seen, Madonna delle Neve. It sits at the bottom of the steps that bring you down to this beach and is sandwiched between the restaurants **Risorgimento** and **Ippocampo**. I have often seen the local fishermen use the wall of this chapel to hang their nets on. But that's okay; they are its protectors and guardians. If you ask nicely at the Ippocampo restaurant, they'll produce the key to the chapel and grant you access. It is a little treasure.

Almost next door to the chapel is **La Tonnarella** (below), a great place for lunch or dinner. Recently when some friends and I were coming back from Amalfi to Positano by boat in the evening, we discovered this little beach in full celebration. It was 23 July and the night of the Festa del Mare (The Festival of the Sea), which was being celebrated in this small paradise with plenty of fish dishes and wine. I think we finally arrived back in Positano at about 4 a.m.!

Close by the Marina di Conca is **Da Claudio Bed and Breakfast**, a delightful cascade of whitewashed rooms that seem to flow down the mountain to the sea. The bar is a busy little shack right on the coastal road with steady passing trade. Claudio's partner Anna cooks the classic *Conchese* dish of rabbit baked in lemon leaves brilliantly, mainly in winter. Da Claudio is also a great well-priced spot to stay in this area.

CONCA

HIKING

One great thing to do in Conca is an easy hike down the pathway that takes you from the Cappella della Madonna delle Lacrime at the top of town to the exit at the fiord of Furore. Along the way you'll see the Grotto delle Monache, which once housed hundreds of bats. At sunset, they would fill the sky like an angry black cloud, giving rise to the name of the pathway, the Sentiero dei Pipistrelli Impazziti (the Pathway of the Crazy Bats). It has to be done, just for the name! According to local friends there are also some great paper mill ruins on this pathway.

POLISPORTIVA

If you are looking for somewhere to eat up in the town, I can highly recommend **Polisportiva**. The entrance is less-than-glamorous, and the interior very local, but this bar, restaurant, gelateria and pizzeria serves up the best of everything.

The first time I visited this place was almost by mistake. I'd been enjoying the view walking this high road and now I was starving, it was late and low season. I put my head through the door and asked if the kitchen was still open, adding quickly that anything would do. A slightly reserved voice asked if *pasta e totani* would be okay. My God, would it! It was one of my favourite dishes: flying squid and pasta. I snuggled into my chair with a glass of red and waited patiently, watching in fascination as the man behind the gelato counter painstakingly scooped *stracciatella* into a line of cones. He very carefully inserted a soaked cherry into the middle of each one and then dipped them in melted chocolate – I knew what I was having for dessert! Both the *totani* and the gelato were out of this world. The gelato-scooper was the owner, nicknamed *Capo* (the boss), and this ice cream was one of his specialties. To top it all off, this restaurant has a tennis court and mini soccer field out the back.

SAINTS AND MADONNAS

With over 230 churches on this 40-kilometre stretch of coastline (that's almost six churches per kilometre), religion plays an important part in the lives of the coast's inhabitants. Every city and town has its own patron saint, and every year people celebrate their saint's day with fireworks, street fairs, feasts, and anything else they can think of to help them celebrate. Work is generally cancelled for the day.

Recently, I was in Positano when the famous Madonna del Rosario was returned to its ancient church in Piazza Mulini after twenty-five years of restoration work in Naples. This little church, La Chiesa del Rosario, which some say is the oldest in Positano dating back to 1000 AD, was shut the entire time she was away. The celebration the day this antique olive-wood statue returned to Positano was phenomenal, and went for days. Boy, when the Catholics kick up their heels, they can outdo any night club on the coast!

The Madonna is the most important religious figure on the Amalfi Coast. She's known by many names: Assunta, Madre, Maria, to mention just a few. She's feted like a movie star all over Italy, but here she's even bigger than that. Her figure appears in niches along the coastal road and is often tucked into bushes all over the mountainside. She can be found on bumper stickers, posters, pamphlets and telephone boxes, and I have even seen her image stuck to a kid's pair of roller skates. She represents Italy's passion and reverence for all things maternal; she is their great protector; she is, without doubt, the most loved woman in the country.

The mother church in Positano contains the legendary black Byzantine Madonna icon. She is carefully removed from the chapel before each major religious event and ceremoniously carried around the town in a procession. The mythical stories of how she came to Positano are numerous and fascinating. My favourite, according to local legend, is that she was stolen from Byzantium by sea-faring Saracens. While passing the Amalfi coastline, a violent storm hit near Positano and the frightened sailors heard a voice calling '*Posa, posa*!' ('Put down, put down!'). They immediately knew this should be the protective home for the black Madonna, so the precious icon was unloaded, carried to the fishing village and laid on the beach, and the sailors then continued their voyage on tranquil seas.

AMALFI, *L'ANTICA REPUBLICA MARITTIMA* (THE ANCIENT MARITIME REPUBLIC) POPULATION: 6000 INHABITANTS: *Amalfitani*
ORIGINS OF THE NAME: There are many stories as to how Amalfi got its name – my favourite is that it was named after a nymph called
Amalfi who was loved and adored by Hercules, and legend has it she was buried in this town; however, the Romans most likely named
it 'Amalphis', after the nearby river 'Malphe' DISTRICTS: Vettica, Lone, Pastena, Pogerola, Tovere PATRON SAINT: Sant' Andrea

Apostolo, protector of the fishermen, celebrated on 30 November MOTHER CHURCH (*CHIESA MADRE*): Sant' Andrea TOWERS: Capo di Vettica or Capo de la Vite (in Vettica), Capo D'Atrani (now a restaurant and hotel) TYPICAL DISH: *Pesce all'acqua pazza – spigola* or sea bass in crazy water (in the days of the Maritime Republic of Amalfi, sailors would cook their fish in sea water, hence the name 'crazy' water)

Apostolo, protector of the fishermen, celebrated on 30 November MOTHER CHURCH (*CHIESA MADRE*): Sant' Andrea TOWERS: Capo di Vettica or Capo de la Vite (in Vettica), Capo D'Atrani (now a restaurant and hotel) TYPICAL DISH: *Pesce all'acqua pazza – spigola* or sea bass in crazy water (in the days of the Maritime Republic of Amalfi, sailors would cook their fish in sea water, hence the name 'crazy' water)

S. ANDREA APOSTOLO

Miracolo succeduto in difesa di Amalfi contro il famoso corsaro Ariadeno Barbarossa nel dì
27-6-1544

'THE DAY OF JUDGEMENT, FOR THOSE AMALFITANIS THAT GO TO HEAVEN, WILL BE A DAY LIKE ANY OTHER!'

RENATO FUCINI, WELL-KNOWN ITALIAN WRITER

FIRST IMPRESSIONS

Until recently, I never really thought about the rich and important history of Amalfi. For me, it was the town in the heart of the Amalfi Coast where most of the teenagers of Positano went to high school, where I had to go to battle over my electricity bills and wait in National Health queues for hours. I would come here to buy dried spices and candied fruit to make *pastiera* Easter cake or to buy delicious *savoiard* chocolate biscuits called *lingue di gatto* (cat's tongues). These biscuits were such a favourite in our family – they often didn't even make it back to Positano, instead being devoured in the car on the way home. Nowadays you can't buy quite the same biscuits, but the pastry shop and bar **Pasticceria Pansa** (established in 1830) sell something very similar called *le tegoline* (little tiles). This should be your breakfast stop, and it's also famous for its great coffee, chocolate-dipped candied fruits and illegally good pastries!

Don't let the busy main piazza of Amalfi scare you when you arrive in town for the first time. You will be confronted with colourful kitsch tea towels, rubber shoes, floral beach bags and an array of sparkly bottles of *limoncello* liqueur on every corner. Just take your time and get into the back streets and stairs that lead to the fascinating hidden corners of the town. It is an enchanting and beautiful city to discover.

My favourite way to get to Amalfi is by sea. Amalfi has the only petrol pump for boats on the Amalfi Coast; otherwise it's all the way to Salerno in one direction or Capri in the other. Amalfi was our supplier. I would love the half-hour boat drive to Amalfi to get petrol with Sergio and the Da Adolfo staff. We would always have a bit of fun in the grottos on the way there or coming home, sometimes even stopping for lunch at Conca or Vettica. Today I still make this trip with Salvatore Capraro when I do his boat tours. Coming to Amalfi on the old ferry is a great way to avoid all that road traffic in peak season and is a beautiful cruise up the coast, where you can enjoy all the magnificent villas and lemon-coloured terraces on the way.

ABOVE: Impeccable service at the bar at Pasticceria Pansa

THE COMPASS

Amalfi boasts the discovery of the compass. But Positano fiercely rejects this idea and claims Flavio Gioia and his compass as theirs. Positano has a piazza named after him and Amalfi has his statue in their main square. Needless to say the two towns continually argue about which town he came from.

But history also suggests that Flavio was mythical and that the compass was simply modified for marine use by a certain Giovanni Gioia in the early 1300s, having already been discovered by China many years earlier. In any case, the compass certainly contributed to the *Amalfitanis'* success with their maritime export and import throughout the Mediterranean Sea.

THE MARITIME REPUBLIC OF AMALFI

Established in the ninth century, the Maritime Republic of Amalfi was a powerful and sophisticated European naval power. Proof of Amalfi's prowess as a great builder of naval and merchant vessels can be seen today in the humble remains of two pathways flanked by ten pillars on the main port, the only surviving example of a medieval shipyard in Italy. Commerce was the speciality of the *Amalfitani*. Their great naval fleets carried goods to the Arab countries where they were traded for gold. They also purchased gems, spices and fine textiles, which they would then sell all over Italy on their return. The *Amalfitani* created colonies around the Mediterranean ports, building houses, shops, factories, churches, monasteries and hospitals. A volume of maritime laws, the Tabula de Amalpha, was established by this powerful city and became widely recognised and adopted. This 66-chapter volume can be viewed today at the Museo Civico (Civic Museum), just behind the cathedral in the Municipal Council. In fact the Republic was so progressive that women had the right to vote during these times.

In the early 1100s, Amalfi lost its independence to the Republic of Pisa: a brutal invasion from the north brought about the destruction of much of Amalfi and its history. The *Amalfitani* survived due to their knowledge of agriculture, leather tanning and manufacturing of paper and cloth. In the seventeenth and eighteenth centuries they turned to pasta production and lemon cultivation. In the mid-nineteenth century, artists, writers, composers and philosophers began to visit Amalfi, drawn to the beauty of the area, and by the mid-twentieth century the post-war tourist boom had started.

AMALFI'S CARTIERES

It is said that paper was invented in China in the first century BC and quickly made its way to the Arab world. Thanks to Amalfi's strong and established commercial ties with this part of the world, their paper-making knowledge was recognised as early as the thirteenth century. But Amalfi's notary lawyers of the time were forbidden by the king of Naples, Federico II, to use this flimsy modern substitute for the more robust parchment. Only as time progressed did the authorities allow documents to be written on the famous Amalfi paper, after verifying its strength and durability. By the fourteenth century, paper mills were cropping up all over the coast and particularly in the Valle dei Mulini (Valley of Windmills) in Amalfi. You can still see the ruins of many of these paper mills when hiking alongside the rivers on the coast.

At the end of the eighteenth century there were sixteen *cartieri* (paper-makers) in the Valle dei Mulini alone and many others up and down the coast. When I first arrived in the area there were several paper manufacturers operating and I would

ABOVE: Stacks of delicate handmade paper at the mills of Amatruda

buy exquisite papers to correspond with friends and family. But in this era of email communication, and due to transport and labour difficulties, there remains but one manufacturer in this lush and cool valley: **Amatruda**.

The magnificent writing paper produced by this manufacturer has a thick, creamy texture and a fibrous edge that appears to have been ironed under a steamroller. It invites a deep ink well and a fine-pointed nib. Well-known artists who use this luxurious paper today have contributed enormously to the continued success of the factory. The Vatican continues to use this paper for correspondence, and occasionally a work of fiction, such as the Tallone Publishing House edition of *Hamlet*, is printed on it. Today the Amatruda factory produces all sizes of this soft, seductive paper from 10 cm × 7 cm business-cards to the artist's sheet size of 100 cm × 70 cm.

If you want to see the old method of paper-making, visit the **Museo della Carta** (Paper Museum), built on the site of an old paper mill. They even have a library containing over 3000 texts that were printed on the original paper.

THE AMALFI REGATTA

The incredible Regata di Amalfi was first held in 1954, and every year since, the former maritime republics of Amalfi, Pisa, Genoa and Venice take part in a rowing competition, showing off their antique and decorative long boats. The regatta takes place on the first Sunday in June, and representatives from the four cities wear traditional costume, each embellished with their symbol: Venice has its lion, Pisa the eagle, Amalfi the horse, and Genoa the mythological griffin-vulture (half lion, half eagle). If you are lucky enough to catch this celebration on the coast (the event moves city each year – the next one in Amalfi will be in 2009), the procession begins on the church steps in Atrani and slowly moves its way through Amalfi followed by a two-kilometre row out to sea.

During my second-ever trip to Positano, I was invited by my friend Patricia Schultz to accompany her to the Amalfi regatta. Schultzie is a travel writer and was working on a coffee-table book on medieval games in Italy. The fabulous mariners' regatta was part of her research. We unloaded our gear into a tiny rented room in Positano and the next morning headed for Amalfi, a half-hour drive away. Surprisingly there was little traffic around and on entering the small port, and not a banner, costume or trumpet was in sight! Unusual for an ancient Italian celebration, we thought. We headed straight to the tourist office and were told that the event had already taken place the weekend before. Schultzie was mortified, realising she would have to wait another year to cover this annual event, and that it would be held on the less-spectacular shoreline of Pisa the following year. Schultzie did eventually get her timing right and went on to write the international bestseller *1000 Places to See Before You Die*.

MANNA FROM SANT' ANDREA

Miracles are a dime a dozen in this part of the world, but Sant' Andrea is a little more curious. A crystal vial is placed on top of Sant' Andrea's burial chamber on the eve of the saint's celebrations (27 June and 30 November). The next day a syrupy liquid called *manna* collects in the vial, which is said to be holy fluid from Sant' Andrea's body, and indicates that the patron saint is happy and will bring fortune to the town and all within it. If the substance does not appear, the year could be a rocky one for the town. Fortunately it usually does what it is supposed to. This celebration day is a very important and spiritual occasion for the *Amalfitani*.

SANT' ANDREA

The Sant' Andrea church, named after the patron saint of Amalfi, is an architectural cocktail – the product of centuries of change – spanning styles from Roman to baroque. I like it – it has something for everyone! Modern-day renovations have minimised the chaos and created a sort of harmony with the simpler Roman exterior. A wander through the belly of this magnificent church not only provides a short cut to a tiny back street but also leads to the offices of a doctor, architect and lawyer, now housed in the foundations of the church. Adjoining are the beautiful Cloisters of Paradise, the VIP burial area. This delightful square garden encases 120 perfect Moorish-style columns surrounded by richly carved sarcophagi.

Make sure you leave enough time to take the organised tour of the church – it's one of the best I've ever done. In less than half an hour you can explore the cathedral, fairytale cloisters and breathtaking crypt, as well as the little museum housed in the former Basilica of the Crucifix, which contains frescos, fabrics, golden *tari'* (coins from the twelfth century), carvings and sculpture. On the other hand, you could linger for hours amongst these treasures if you have time.

The official day of celebration for Sant' Andrea is 30 November, but he is so important he is also celebrated on 27 June. The story goes that Andrea saved the *Amalfitani* 500 years ago by creating a terrifying storm, which frightened off the invading Barbarossa. The celebration is a wonderful sight, with locals dressing up in traditional costumes and proceeding through the town. Hang around till the end and you will see robust locals haul Sant' Andrea's hefty silver statue up the steep cathedral stairs – at a gallop. A sight not to be missed.

VILLA ROMANA

When Barbara, my English friend who has been an Amalfi local since 1968, said she would take me to see the Roman villa in Amalfi, I envisaged a climb over vine-covered rocks with small bubbling streams and crumbling stone statues scattered among the vegetation. Instead she led me through a large neon-lit ceramic shop called **Il Ninfeo**, and simply said to the shop assistant, 'La villa Romana, per favore,' and the salesgirl walked over to a stairwell, flicked a switch and gestured for us to walk down. No payment, no questions, just a Roman villa! We entered a large square room with a glass floor – this was the courtyard garden of the villa. Around the room were mist-covered glass cases displaying fascinating vases and metal objects that had been discovered. All in all an interesting diversion if you are wandering down the main street of Amalfi on your way to pick up your pasta or buy some shoes.

OPPOSITE: It's hard to decide which is more spectacular – the exterior or the interior of the wonderful Sant' Andrea church

EXPLORING THE VALLE DEI MULINI

Also known as the Valle delle Ferriere (Ironmongers' Valley), this valley was celebrated by the great artists and writers of the 1800s for its natural beauty. A short walk from Amalfi will bring you to the edge of this splendid valley that has been an inspiration to many famous artists and writers over the centuries. With its rare prehistoric ferns known as *Woodwardia radicans* or *Felce bulbifera*, its enticing dappled light and fresh-smelling undergrowth, this valley is a trekker's paradise. You need an authorised guide (again I recommend Frank Carpegna), but a two-to-three-hour hike through this magnificent valley, finishing with lunch among the *sfusato* lemon groves of Amalfi, is the perfect 'non-boating' day out on the Amalfi Coast.

EATING AND DRINKING

Good friend and Amalfi native Peppino Amendola is a discerning fish eater (he eats it every day of his life), and **Ristorante Pesce d'Oro** is his favourite place to do it. This is a simple trattoria-style restaurant that has been serving up excellent fresh fish for forty-odd years. The restaurant is on the Amalfi Coast road, just back towards Positano in the district of Vettica.

It's an institution in Amalfi, but the restaurant **La Caravella** really does rate a mention. They boast an excellent seafood-based menu at heart-stopping prices, with wines to match. It is definitely a 'special occasion' night out – wear your tiara so you can impress the sometimes chilly waiters.

I was lucky enough to meet Ezio Falcone, an Amalf-born gastronomic historian, before he died. Ezio's favourite pizzeria in town was on the beach at **Stella Maris**, and for a no-holds-barred seafood lunch down on the beach he recommended **Marina Grande**.

My favourite way to end the day in Amalfi is at **Bar Francese**, opposite the Sant' Andrea church. When the last of the sun's rays light up the church, you can sit in the shade of the bar, Campari in hand, and marvel at the beauty of this jewel-like façade.

FAVOURITE PLACES TO STAY

A simple, pretty and not over-the-top *pensione* in Amalfi is **Hotel La Conchiglia**, right at the end of the port. The biggest bonus here is their parking for guests (finding parking in Amalfi is like finding a palm tree in the Arctic). They also have good beach access in this little corner of the port.

For an upmarket treat, a stay at the famous five-star **Hotel Santa Caterina** (below right) is unbeatable. When I first visited Amalfi, this hotel was quite run-down, but has since been given a fantastic facelift. Their tiny chapel-like suite perched over the sea in the middle of the lemon groves is the ultimate honeymooners' haven.

For the cathedral-crazy, the **Hotel Centrale**, right opposite the imposing Sant' Andrea church, cannot be beaten. This delightfully small and immaculate hotel is clean, neat and very well-priced, and has without a doubt the best view of the cathedral from its breakfast terrace on the top floor (below). If I had a penny for every photograph taken from this terrace . . .

OPPOSITE: The hotel Il Saraceno is extremely humble-looking at street level, but cascades spectacularly down to the beach

BIKES

From the moment I arrived in Italy I seemed to spend a hell of a lot of time on motorbikes. They are just the best way to get around a big city or a crowded holiday resort. I soon bought my own old rust bucket and quickly learnt to ride it.

Buzzing around a big city on a motorbike was usually pretty exciting (and highly stressful!), but never as thrilling as on the Amalfi Coast, with its steep, windy roads and amazing, distracting views. On holiday in Positano, one of my first rides with Sergio was back to my little *pensione* very early one morning just as the sun was coming up. It was August, and the air was still and already very warm. Wearing no helmet, I climbed onto Sergio's massive old Benelli bike in my short skirt, and he pushed off without starting the motor (he would have woken up the entire town had he started the bike up – she was a real growler). With the wind caressing our faces we glided down through this fairytale village, all the way from the top of the mountain down to sea level. I hugged Sergio like a baby koala and, at that moment, fell totally in love with him.

Soon after, Sergio came to visit me in Florence. Returning from work one day, I found my moped on the terrace of my apartment, totally dismantled, with Sergio lovingly cleaning each part and putting it all back together again. I had no idea how he had carried this bike up two flights of stairs – it weighed a ton. The bike went like a treat after this surgery, and I was convinced that Sergio was the man for me (he had used his last 20 000 lire to buy the few spare parts he needed for the bike, *and* cooked me his father's signature dish Pollo Adolfo, a delicious meal of chicken with black olives … I was a goner!).

Once I moved to Positano, I upgraded to a 'real', geared bike. One warm summer's evening, I was confidently riding my GB Uno to a swish cocktail party at Le Sirenuse, wearing a new floaty silk skirt. As I passed the hotel entrance to park my bike, my billowing skirt caught in the bike chain and was ripped off my body. The porters watched in fascination, and I learnt the hard way that evening wear and bikes just don't mix.

Sergio taught me to ride safely on the difficult roads of the Amalfi Coast, but please don't hire a bike on your holidays unless you are a very proficient rider. I have seen so many young (and not-so-young) tourists come to grief against a mountain wall – a bad way to end a holiday. Marco has been nagging me since he was fourteen to let him get his *patentino* (little licence) to drive a 50 cc motorbike in Italy – amazingly, this is the legal age. It seems absurd, but until a short time ago, fourteen-year-olds could actually drive one of these zippy little things without any licence at all… another reason to be careful!

ATRANI, *IL PIU' PICCOLO COMUNE DELL' ITALIA MERIDIONALE* (THE SMALLEST MUNICIPALITY IN SOUTHERN ITALY) POPULATION: 950
INHABITANTS: *Atranesi* ORIGINS OF THE NAME: Atrani is named for its geographic situation – occupying a slit in the Lattari Mountains,
the town derives its name from the Latin term atrum, meaning dark PATRON SAINT: Santa Maria Maddelena, protector of hairdressers,
prostitutes and the repentant, celebrated on 22 July

'DOWN THERE, THOSE BIZARRE IDEAS CAME TO ME ABOUT BIRDS, FISH, SKIES, WATERS.'

M.C. ESCHER, ON THE WAY ATRANI INSPIRED HIS ART IN THE 1920S

A PRECIOUS LITTLE PLACE

Atrani is the smallest commune in Italy – in fact in all of Europe, according to some guidebooks. It does not even cover one square kilometre. The first time you arrive in this little paradise of whitewashed houses, you'll feel like you've walked onto a film set. Atrani is known today as one of the *borghi piu belli d'italia*, the most beautiful villages of Italy. Aesthetically it has always been my favourite village on the Amalfi Coast – after Positano, of course.

In high summer, when the car park on the beach is full and the road in town is closed to traffic, the best way to get to Atrani is by walking along a gentle pathway that connects the town to Amalfi. The path hugs the hillside, providing beautiful views of the sea as it weaves through Atrani's whitewashed houses. The walk takes 20–30 minutes.

AN EVENING AT CHEZ CHECCO

The first time I visited Atrani it was a warm summer's night, lit only by the full moon which illuminated the white houses, arches and balconies of this coastal nest. I couldn't wait to come back during the day. Sandrina, my dear friend from Praiano, and her boyfriend were taking us to a very special dinner at the restaurant/club Chez Checco, nestled in one of the many narrow streets of this charming village. As we wandered up the cobblestone street, following the smell of melted mozzarella and baked eggplant, all we could hear were the gentle rhythmic waves brushing over the stones on the beach behind us.

Sandrina was a good friend of Checco's, and not only did he open the restaurant exclusively for us, he and his wife prepared a fabulous dinner and amused us with colourful stories from the heyday of this club, which was the first nightclub on the Amalfi Coast. 'Jackie Kennedy Onassis would dance on the tables! She loved this place,' he said. Sadly Chez Checco is now closed and he and his wife are no longer with us, but beware – a well-known guidebook still recommends you eat there.

OPPOSITE: The impressive Santa Maria Maddelena church, perched on a spectacular curve of the road

A PROTECTED NICHE

When the Maritime Republic of Amalfi was at the height of its power, Atrani, on Amalfi's eastern border, was the enclave of the nobility and the republic's religious centre. This very special little area had over 300 churches and private chapels. As far west as Capri and as far east as Vietri, including the villages of the Lattari Mountains, the people were all known as *Amalfitani* – the residents of Atrani, however, were still known as *Atranesi*.

After the brutal collapse of the Maritime Republic in 1135–1137, when the Pisano arrived from the north, burning and ransacking the entire region, things did not get any better on the coast. The great *mare motto*, or tidal wave, of 1343 destroyed a significant part of this town and many others along the way. And in 1643 the plague wiped out what little was left.

The coastal road curves through Atrani, crossing over the top of the entire town. It has formed a type of protective barrier, making Atrani the most untouched village on the coast. It has helped the town retain more of its original features and authenticity than any other in the area.

Dominating the most spectacular curve in town is the church built in honour of Atrani's patron saint, Santa Maria Maddelena. Its majolica-tiled dome resembles that of the mother church of Positano, Maria Assunta, and it has a beautiful 1500s bell tower and rococo façade.

The baroque church of Sant Salvatore de' Birecto, built around 1100, is another must-see. Its rich bronze doors are a testament to the generosity extended towards the church at this time. Inside the church is a spectacular marble bas-relief pluteum – a dividing panel which separates the altar area from the rest of the church. This bas-relief depicts two stylised peacocks separated by a tree, and dates back to the Byzantine era.

The wonderful thing about Atrani is that everything is just a stone's throw away: the churches you want to visit, the meals you want to eat, the coffee you want to sip in the piazza in the morning sun, or the dip you want to take before lunch at the beach. Everything, that is, except the church of Santa Maria del Bando (left) and the best view of the town. To get to this chalk-white gem perched on the hillside, you must climb 500 steps (no, you can't drive). Legend has it that it was from this little tenth-century treasure, with its acoustically perfect position, that court sentences were handed down to the townsfolk.

Peccati di gola

6

EATING AND DRINKING

One of my very favourite places to eat on the Amalfi Coast is **Ristorante A'Paranza** in Atrani. Sergio and I would try to eat there as often as we could in the low season, when we could get away from Laurito. The two brothers who own this restaurant, Massimo and Roberto, are masters of their trade.

If you are travelling by car, you may find a traffic warden at the entrance of town saying, '*Il paese é pieno*' ('The town is full'). If you have booked at A'Paranza (which I suggest you always do), then keep their phone number handy and give them a call – they will most likely be able to sort it out and get you in.

Like many restaurants in this area, A'Paranza pride themselves on incredible antipasti. Most are seafood-based and all are delicious: rolled, grilled or stuffed squid with provolone cheese; perfectly char-grilled baby octopus; stewed calamari with potatoes fried in oil and parsley; diced mussels baked in a gratin. In this cavern-style restaurant your view is sacrificed, but it's worth it for the chance to enjoy these delicacies, one after another. Beware, though, that if you overindulge in the antipasto you will never fit in the yummy homemade pasta or the creamy seafood risotto. A'Paranza also does excellent desserts, so pace yourself.

There are two fabulous bars right in the heart of Atrani that I never miss visiting for an aperitif before lunch or dinner or a good espresso after. **Bar Birecto** and **La Risacca** are both in the main piazza, and offer snacks, great coffee and drinks until late into the night, and cater to a mix of locals and foreigners.

OTHER FAVOURITE THINGS

The quickest and easiest-access swim on the Amalfi Coast is here in Atrani. The beach (opposite) is practically part of the car park, or down a short staircase from the Amalfi Coast road if coming by bus, and the water is generally crystal-clear and divine. You swim in an amphitheatre of antiquity – just heaven!

There is no five-star accommodation in Atrani; for that you will have to stay in nearby Amalfi. But **A'Scalinatella** is a backpacker's paradise, or you could try one of Eva Caruso's three delightful little rooms above Zaccaria restaurant, each overlooking the sea. Alternatively, **L'Argine Fiorito** is a cute bed-and-breakfast with six rooms but no sea views.

If you are lucky enough to be in town at the end of August, don't miss the Sagra del Pesce Azzurro (Deep Sea Fish Festival). You can savour anchovies and tuna fried or grilled on the main beach in the evening, all washed down with plenty of good local wine. It makes a great summer's night out.

157

ABOVE: The large mural on the wall of Ristorante A'Paranza

WEATHER AND WINDS

The livelihoods of the Amalfi Coast inhabitants are heavily dependent on the weather – in the high season, good weather is crucial to most activities on the coast. Listen carefully to the locals and you'll pick up some tips; they discuss the weather constantly. Understanding the winds and how they affect weather patterns will help you make the most of your holiday; you'll know when to book your boat trip, do a mountain walk, or just stay in bed with a good book.

Here are a few pointers about the most talked-about winds in this area:

Sirocco
Brings very warm, sometimes hot, weather. The sea can get quite rough and if it rains, it rains red dust. Bad for boating.

Libeccio
Brings bad weather with very rough seas, which can last up to 3–4 days.

Tramontana
A freezing, strong wind direct from the North Pole, which usually brings clear, crisp weather. Most common in January and February, but can occur suddenly at other times.

Mistrale
A warm breeze (sometimes bloody strong too!) which usually signals great weather for the next day if it appears in the latter part of the afternoon. Great for windsurfing and sailing.

Levante
Usually brings good weather if it's around in the morning, but bad weather if it appears in the evening.

Ponente
Brings fine weather, so get out there and enjoy it!

Grecale
Brings bad weather if around all day; if spasmodic can mean changing weather ahead.

RAVELLO, *LA CITTÀ DELLA MUSICA* (THE CITY OF MUSIC) POPULATION: 2500 INHABITANTS: *Ravellesi* ORIGINS OF THE NAME: Rabellum or Ravellum – referring to the nobles who rebelled against the Maritime Republic of Amalfi by moving up the mountain DISTRICTS: Castiglione, Sambuco, Torello, San Martino-Monte

PATRON SAINT: San Pantaleone, protector of medics, celebrated on 27 July **MOTHER CHURCH** (*CHIESA MADRE*): Duomo of San Pantaleone
TOWER: Torre dello Scarpariello **TYPICAL DISH:** *Pollo con i pepperoni e zucchini fritti* (chicken with capsicum and fried zucchini)

'NEARER TO THE SKY THAN IT IS TO THE SHORE.'

ANDRÉ GIDE, NOBEL PRIZE-WINNING FRENCH AUTHOR

APPROACHING RAVELLO

Sitting high up in the Lattari Mountains, Ravello catches the warm breezes from the south-east that deliver the perfume of every native flower in the surrounding area. From Positano it's a half-hour drive down the coast, passing through bustling Amalfi and the perfect miniature town of Atrani, then at the next bend, take a hard left at a large mural of a mythological *pistrice,* half beast, half fish, which stares back at you with one large black eye. The fifteen-minute drive around numerous blind corners that follows is not for the faint-hearted; however, a traffic-light system has recently been devised to allow only one side to pass at a time. Nevertheless, have your hand ready on the horn, as the locals do. Once you arrive, there is a small parking tariff to pay, but a fairytale village awaits you.

Ravello not only occupies a magnificent open-air terrace by the sea, it is also the cultural centre of the Amalfi Coast, and has long been a favourite destination for artists, musicians and writers. But today there is little to keep the young folk up here; in fact, you see them flying at lightning speed down the narrow windy hillside on their motorbikes, on their way to the noisier and more vibrant city of Amalfi. But for a tranquil, relaxing holiday, Ravello is perfect.

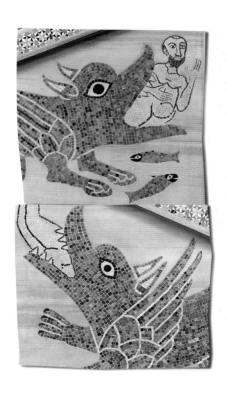

THE DUOMO OF RAVELLO

The Duomo of Ravello is named after the patron saint of the town, San Pantaleone, and was built around 1086. It holds a beautiful and much-photographed Byzantine pulpit from 1290 in its main nave and another stunning marble pulpit from the Roman era. Although this cathedral has undergone many transformations through the centuries, today it is close to its original Roman state.

165

ABOVE: *Pistrice* mosaics in the Duomo of Ravello

THE MUSIC FESTIVAL AND VILLA RUFOLO

For me, the true attraction of Ravello is the Wagner music festival which runs throughout summer. Concerts are held mostly in the evening, in beautiful gardens, piazzas and palaces scattered throughout the town.

The spectacular thirteenth-century **Villa Rufolo** (left), with its pristine cascading gardens, is one of the venues for the festival. Originally owned by the Rufolo family, it was bought and beautifully restored by the Scotsman Francis Neville Reid in the mid-1800s. Although its two towers, which combine Sicilian, Arabic and Norman styles, are famous, they can't match the splendour of the view from the villa itself of the Lattari Mountains above and the Amalfi coastline below. When Richard Wagner visited Ravello at the end of the 1800s, he was so taken with the amazing vista from these gardens that he reputedly exclaimed, 'Finally the magical garden of Klingsor has been found!', referring to an important scene from *Parsifal*, the opera he was working on. The Ravello Festival began in the mid-fifties as a tribute to Wagner, and still flourishes today, embracing a variety of sounds for music lovers. You can hear anything from an international philharmonic orchestra playing Wagner, Strauss, Rossini or Gershwin, to the contemporary sounds of Herbie Hancock, while gazing out over this celestial panorama – it's a once-in-a-lifetime experience.

Many years ago I took my mother Maggie and her best friend Barbara up to Ravello for an evening philharmonic concert. As always, the concert was to begin at sunset, and while the 130-piece orchestra was warming up onstage and the audience were taking their seats, there was a sense that something magical was about to happen. I turned to look at my mother gazing down on the coastline and saw tears rolling down her cheek. When I looked the other way, I realised that Barbara was crying too. The orchestra had not yet struck a note, but the atmosphere was emotionally charged. Attending a concert at this festival is one of the most unforgettable evenings you could ever experience on the coast.

WEDDINGS

Another popular thing to do in Ravello is get married! The head priest, Monsignor Giuseppe Imperato (known to all as Don Peppino) must have one very full wedding diary, as people come from all over the world to get married here – the church steps are well worn from brides' heels. If you are not Catholic, there are plenty of other breathtaking venues to choose from.

The magnificent **Villa Cimbrone** is a must-see and is also a wonderful place to get married. This eleventh-century villa, which has been occupied by noblemen,

OPPOSITE: Beautifully decorated columns inside the Duomo of Ravello

OVERLEAF: The dream-like Villa Cimbrone and its famous statue-studded gardens

kings and princes, really came into its own in the early twentieth century when Ernest William Beckett – later to become Lord Grimthorpe – took possession of it. He set out to make Cimbrone and its surroundings 'the most beautiful place in the world', and it became a haven for many prominent artists, writers and statesmen. Salvador Dalí, D.H. Lawrence, Gianni Agnelli, Virginia Woolf and Winston Churchill all stayed at this villa at one time or another. Today it is run as a five-star hotel, and is still renowned for its magnificent terrace and its lush manicured park studded with impressive statues.

For a beautiful, professionally organised wedding in a fairytale garden, the **Villa Eva**, just next door to Cimbrone, is another excellent spot. And if money is no object, the newly renovated **La Rondinaia** (which up until recently was owned by Gore Vidal), could be the treat of a lifetime. This unique villa hangs suspended over the Amalfi Coast and is a gentle walk from the main part of town. It sleeps twenty, so you can put up the entire wedding party here, and with personal service, its own restaurant and five-star spa, it is sheer luxury.

CAMEOS

While exploring the villas and backstreets of this wonderful town with my mother Maggie recently, our first stop was an iconic jewellery shop that sells incredible cameos, corals and turquoise, **The Cameo Factory**. Neither of us is a cameo girl, but the large coral beads threaded into a long necklace in the window grabbed our attention. While Mum moved around the store admiring its beautiful pieces I struck up a conversation with the owner, Giorgio Camo, who was seated behind his workbench strewn with numerous ancient cameo-crafting tools. Elegantly dressed in cream linen, and with an impressive walking cane resting close by, he gave the impression of having stepped straight out of a Visconti film. Giorgio told me that he had owned and run this shop for nearly forty years. He gave us a rundown on coral in this area – apparently it is almost impossible now to find the beautiful large chunks of coral required to make a necklace such as the one in the window. Meanwhile my eyes wandered over pictures of the many famous faces on the walls. Giorgio told us that Hillary Clinton is among his regular customers.

He insisted we inspect the small coral museum at the back of the store, which opened twenty-odd years ago and has since become quite an attraction. He showed us his centuries-old religious icons and filigree delicacies, some dating as far back as Roman times. Among his treasures are a seventeenth-century crucifix, a beautiful Madonna figure from the mid-1500s and a Roman amphora. Each piece is beautifully inlaid with coral or shell. While he was showing us around, Giorgio kept discreetly looking at the very long strand of turquoise I was wearing. Before we left he delicately told me that they were not real turquoise but made with turquoise paste. I was crushed!

BRIC-A-BRAC
Also in the main piazza of Ravello is *the* bric-a-brac shop of the area. This labyrinthine store sells everything from beautiful handmade writing paper from Amalfi to wrought-iron bedheads and antique tables and tiles. It is a great place to spend an hour or two wandering around, and they'll ship goods anywhere in the world.

OPPOSITE: Some well-worn cameo-making tools at The Cameo Factory

EATING AND DRINKING

One of my old haunts from the early days is the famous **Cumpà Cosimo**, just a short walk down a sidestreet from the main piazza. Owned and run by Netta and Luca Bottone, the restaurant has been going for 79 years. This family knows about food, eating and how to run a restaurant. Netta bustles among the diners, taking orders, while the kitchen offers hearty and wholesome local cuisine, specialising in homemade pasta. They do not hold back on the oil or condiments, so if you are dieting, all the worse for you! There is no view and no fancy trimmings, just good, wholesome, honest food. You don't have to worry too much about a menu because Netta will most likely tell you what you are going to eat – she doesn't mess around! And believe me, you will wish you'd only had an espresso for breakfast.

I always go to **Caffè Calce**, right next to the cathedral, for a good coffee and *cornetto* (croissant) as soon as I arrive. I like the white-linen feel of this bar – it's quite chi-chi. Over the years I have tried all the bars in this piazza, and Caffè Calce is the best, with good service, good coffee and a decent loo – always a treat in Italy!

Just down the road from Cimbrone is **Villa Maria**, a cosy hotel and a favourite lunchtime spot for the view from the cool, shaded terrace. And I'm not the only person who thinks so. During my first lunch at Villa Maria, I spotted a table of eleven robed Dominican monks enjoying a noisy and happy meal accompanied by several carafes of red wine. Villa Maria is also known for its *pasta tagliatelle con i porcini* (pasta with porcini mushrooms), and its wonderful organic vegetables, grown right next door to the restaurant.

The owner of Villa Maria, Vincenzo Palumbo – 'Professore' to friends – once introduced me to the charming Ezio Falcone, an Amalfi-born native whose business card read 'Historical Cooking's Teacher'. Ezio was a consultant on historical and traditional cuisine along the entire Amalfi Coast and collaborated with many of the top hotels, contributing to their cooking schools through the year. The author of several books on the subject, he was particularly interested in continuing the culinary traditions of each area, and one of his most frequented spots for these courses was at Villa Maria. He would explain the origins of the ingredients and the traditional methods behind each recipe, while the hotel's chefs guided you through the practical steps.

OPPOSITE: This delightful table at Cumpà Cosimo is reserved for regulars or friends who just drop in for a meal. I ate with a dozen different people on this visit!

FIVE-STAR HOTEL HEAVEN

The choice of five-star hotels in this magical town is almost embarrassing. Most are housed in former noble palaces, built in a row, and boast heavenly views, glorious gardens, luxury service and total tranquillity.

My favourite is the beautiful and traditional **Hotel Palumbo**, originally called Villa Episcopio. I have enjoyed many wonderful lunches in the restaurant with its high frescoed ceilings, while gazing down on the blue Mediterranean. It is easy to see why this hotel was a favourite with the likes of Richard Wagner, Tennessee Williams, Truman Capote, Gore Vidal, and the Danish royal family. Every nook and cranny of this delightful hotel suggests a wonderful adventure or a story to tell.

Palumbo has two well-known neighbours. **Palazzo Sasso** is a recently refurbished, twelfth-century, pretty pink structure with Moorish arches. During much of the twentieth century this was known as Hotel Palumbo and owned by the Viullmieur family, who still own and run the current Hotel Palumbo next door.

On the other side of Sasso is the classic **Hotel Caruso**. Originally an eleventh-century palace, it boasts delicate floral frescos in its ground-floor boutique and a magnificent portal (below) at its entrance, believed to have been removed from the nearby church of Sant' Eustachio in Scala during the sixteenth century, when the villa owners also owned the church. It even has its own tiny chapel from the same era on one of the upper levels.

SCALA, *IL PAESE PIU ANTICO DELLA COSTA D'AMALFI* (THE OLDEST SETTLEMENT ON THE COAST) POPULATION: 1500 INHABITANTS: *Scalesi* ORIGINS OF THE NAME: Scala means stairway (from afar, the town resembles a stairway descending the slope); in ancient times it was known as Cama, which means protected by walls, for its fortifications DISTRICTS: Minuta, Santa Caterina, San Pietro,

Campidolio, Pontone **PATRON SAINT:** San Lorenzo, protector of chefs and firemen, celebrated on 10 August **MOTHER CHURCH** (*CHIESA MADRE*)**:** San Lorenzo **TOWER:** Torre dello Ziro **TYPICAL DISHES:** The ancient dish of spelt with beans, or the more modern vermicelli with cheese and eggs

'THE DOORWAY TO PARADISE IS ALMOST A METAPHYSICAL STAIRWAY THAT CARRIES YOU UPWARDS AND HOLDS YOU SUSPENDED IN AN INFINITE CONTEMPLATION.'

ANDRÉ GIDE, NOBEL PRIZE-WINNING FRENCH AUTHOR

OPEN AIR AND PEACE FOR THE SOUL

Perched 400 metres above Atrani and Amalfi, and one kilometre from Ravello, Scala has none of the hectic traffic of the coastal towns. Along with only four other communes in the region of Campania, Scala has joined the prestigious Villaggi d'Europa group of gem-like rural villages in Europe. It is the perfect destination to relax and recharge.

Scala is the oldest settlement on the Amalfi Coast. It was founded some time in the fourth century by Romans shipwrecked on their way to Constantinople. With its elevated position providing a telescopic view of the comings and goings below, and its flanks well protected by the glorious Lattari Mountains, it was the ideal location for a Roman settlement. Together with Ravello, Scala became an important fortification for the Duchy of Amalfi during the era of the Maritime Republic. It housed and protected many of the noble families from aggressive invaders. Like Amalfi, Scala flourished economically and commercially at this time, and a large number of churches, palaces and protective walls were constructed. In fact, it is said that at one time Scala possessed close to one hundred churches. Today there are fifteen – still a considerable number, given that the population is only about 1500.

SCALA

CHESTNUT HARVEST

As in so many mountain communities in the area, the second and third week of October is the time for the chestnut harvest. This is celebrated with weekend street fairs where you can sample chestnut stews, pies and pastries. Or my favourite: chestnuts simply roasted in their skins in a copper pan over an open fire. Delicious!

DAIRY PRODUCE

Scala boasts some wonderful dairy products. In ancient times only the nobles could afford meat, so the masses got their protein from seasoned and fresh cheeses. Today you'll find plenty of delicious fresh goat-, sheep- and cow's-milk cheeses here, and the **Latteria Santa Caterina** sells some of the best local dairy produce around.

ROCK CLIMBING

If you are interested in rock climbing, there are plenty of climbing areas throughout this mountainous village, all with spectacular views of the coast. **Oreste Bottiglieri** is the local expert and can point you in the right direction.

ABOVE: **My girlfriend Federica and I after a day's riding through the woods of Scala**

OVERLEAF: The Torre dello Ziro, where the Duchess of Malfi was apparently executed in the early 1500s

THE TORRE DELLO ZIRO AND THE DUCHESS OF MALFI

The Torre dello Ziro, which gazes down on Atrani, Amalfi and the wide open waters of the Mediterranean, was built in 1480 on the ruins of another tower from the twelfth century. Legend has it that this beautiful cylindrical tower was where the widowed Giovanna d'Aragona, formerly the Duchess of Malfi, and daughter of the king of Naples Ferdinando I, was exiled by her brothers in about 1510. She had been married to the Duke of Malfi, Alfonso Piccolomini, when she was just twelve years old. They had two children before she was widowed at the age of twenty, when she was left to rule the town. Antonio Bologna, a cultured butler of the dukedom, soon stole the heart of the beautiful duchess. They married in secret and had three children. Eventually they fled to the north, where Giovanna's angry brothers had them followed. Antonio was found in Milan and murdered, and Giovanna was brought back to Amalfi and locked in the Torre dello Ziro with her children. She was executed shortly after. Poor Giovanna was known as *La Pazza* (The Crazy One).

This saga inspired John Webster's seventeenth-century tragedy *The Duchess of Malfi*, the Spanish writer Lope de Vega's *The Duchess of Amalfi's Butler*, and most recently *The Mystery of the Duchess of Malfi*, written by Barbara Banks.

RIDING AROUND SCALA

In my early years on the Amalfi Coast, we would come to Scala in the dead of winter to go horse riding. Bartolo (right) would hire out horses for a day's ride in the woods around Scala. I grew up riding horses in Australia – usually small Arab ponies with fire in their eyes and motor pistons in their legs so that you needed your wits about you just to stay on. But here we rode Bartolo's docile mules and mountain horses. The first time he saw me astride one of his mules, nervously glued to my saddle, he nearly fell off his horse laughing. Rugged up in ski jackets and gloves, we would head off through the scented woods around Scala. Bartolo would leisurely lead us, whispering gently over his shoulder, 'Give him his head; he knows this terrain much better than you do.' And he was right. There was no need to steer or pull up with these mules. It was a matter of just sitting and being led up and down steep, narrow paths through the thick luscious woods. And when we reached the plateau at the top of the mountain range, these mules would gallop like no other horse I have ever known!

Nowadays Bartolo breeds mules only as working animals and doesn't hire them out for riding. But you don't need to be on horseback to explore the chestnut woods and wonderful trails in this area.

BASILICA DI SANT' EUSTACHIO

A must-see in Scala is the stunning, almost contemporary-looking, twelfth-century ruins of the Basilica di Sant' Eustachio (right). This was considered the largest church in the dukedom and is overflowing with fine frescos and solid marble fittings. If you don't feel like the walk down to the church, there is a magnificent view of it from the quaint district of Minuta.

EATING AND DRINKING

For a good home-cooked lunch after riding or hiking, we would often settle into the dining room of the simple hotel restaurant **Zi'Ntonio**. The owner Michele Ferrigno serves good hearty comfort food, most of which comes from his own farm, using local vegetables, local cheeses, local wines and often local meats. Their chicken with wine and herbs is delicious.

On the other side of town, **Da Lorenzo** focuses on fish in summer and meat in winter, a very common thing in these mountainous regions. Their wood-fired oven-baked bread is delicious, as are their local seafood pasta dishes.

If you are trekking in the medieval district of Pontone (part of the Valle delle Ferriere in Amalfi) where the fabulous ruins of Eustachio are found, a meal at the **Trattoria Antico Borgo** is the perfect stop to fuel up. They specialise in wholesome homemade pastas, *a tris* being their signature dish: ravioli with smoked provolone and ricotta; gnocchi or *scialatielli* with porcini mushrooms; and ravioli or gnocchi usually in a fresh tomato and basil sauce. And naturally, they do terrific local rabbit as well.

USES FOR PIG'S BLOOD
Another specialty to try in Scala (if you can find it) is their famous pasta with pig's blood sauce. Traditionally every edible part of the pig was consumed – including the blood, which was boiled down to a solid pudding-like consistency and then added to various dishes. The pasta dish is made by simply frying a chopped onion in olive oil and adding chunks of pig's blood. It has a strong, gamey, interesting flavour. Another delicacy is their *sanguinaccio*, a dessert also created with pig's blood. Thankfully, in this dish there is more chocolate and pine nuts than pig's blood!

SCALA

CHURCHES TO VISIT

Scala's mother church, the twelfth-century cathedral of San Lorenzo (left), was rebuilt in the eighteenth century in baroque style. It has a magnificent majolica floor, which depicts the Scala coat of arms, with a proud lion on a ladder. Its crypt houses two important treasures from the past: a highly decorated mausoleum for Marinella Rufolo (of Ravello's Villa Rufolo fame) that dates from the 1300s; and a two-metre wooden sculpture of Christ on the cross from the thirteenth century.

Santa Annunziata in Minuta holds many magnificent works of art from the Romanesque period which are considered some of the most important in the south of Italy. But for me the real joy of this church is the splendid crypt with its exquisite frescos. It is well worth a visit.

Before leaving Scala, I like to stop and reflect for a moment at the little Grotto of the Revelation, where San Alfonso Maria dei Liguori (author of over 800 books) would isolate himself every so often to talk with the Madonna. This is the perfect town for spiritual discussions.

MINORI, *LA CITTÀ DEL GUSTO* (THE CITY OF FLAVOUR) POPULATION: 3000 INHABITANTS: *Minoresi* ORIGINS OF THE NAME: Both Minori and Maiori were originally called Reghinna after the Etruscan leader who ruled these lands; Minori eventually became Reghinna Minor to differentiate it from Maiori DISTRICTS: Borgo di Villamena, Torre, Petrito, Monte PATRON SAINT: San Trofimena, celebrated on 13 July, 5 November and 27 November

MINORI, *LA CITTÀ DEL GUSTO* (THE CITY OF FLAVOUR) POPULATION: 3000 INHABITANTS: *Minoresi* ORIGINS OF THE NAME: Both Minori and Maiori were originally called Reghinna after the Etruscan leader who ruled these lands; Minori eventually became Reghinna Minor to differentiate it from Maiori DISTRICTS: Borgo di Villamena, Torre, Petrito, Monte PATRON SAINT: San Trofimena, celebrated on 13 July, 5 November and 27 November

MOTHER CHURCH (*CHIESA MADRE*): San Trofimena TOWERS: Torre Paradiso and Torre Mezzacapo TYPICAL DISH: *N'dunderi di ricotta* – once made with spelt and rennet, these mouthwatering gnocchi-type dumplings are made today with Saracen flour and ricotta; they are best served simply with fresh *piennolo* tomato sauce and white pepper

'MINORI, THAT EDEN OF THE COASTLINE, ENJOYS A FRESH AND VENTILATED ATMOSPHERE THAT CALMS THE HEAT OF THE SUMMER SEASON. THE PERFUMED AIR FROM A MYRIAD OF ORANGE AND LEMON FLOWERS DURING SPRING LIFTS THE SPIRIT AND GIVES THE SOUL AN INEXPRESSIBLE SENSUAL PLEASURE.'

MATTEO CAMERA, AMALFI COAST HISTORIAN

CITY OF FLAVOUR

Minori is known as the Città del Gusto (City of Flavour), and almost everything here revolves around food. It is hard to talk or think about anything else as you pass through the candy-coloured town.

The history of Minori and its renowned pasta-making goes back to medieval times and centres around the Reghinna Minor river. Numerous windmills generated the power to grind the grain into flour, and the pasta produced from this flour gained a reputation throughout Italy. The old fountain on the seafront (right), called the Fontana di California for its sunny position, is where generations of pasta-makers would dry their hand-rolled pasta on racks, giving it a salty tang from the sea air. Although today you'll no longer see pasta-makers wandering around the town covered in flour, or the small seafront covered with pasta drying in the sun, you can still buy the famous Minori-made pasta at **Il Pastaio**.

Scialatielli, thick ribbons of fresh pasta, was long assumed to be a specialty of Minori. Not so long ago it seemed that every restaurant on the entire coast was coming to Minori for their supply – the coast road was blocked from morning to night. But it didn't take long before people worked out the exact ingredients and method for making the pasta, and were able to produce their own.

However, according to local food historian Ezio Falcone, a well-known chef at the famous Amalfi Caravella Restaurant originally brought back the recipe for *scialatielli* from Calabria in the 1960s, and reproduced it in this famous restaurant. So it seems this delicacy did not originate in Minori after all . . .

GUSTAMINORI

For one week in early September, Minori is transformed into one giant food fair. Gustaminori is a renowned open-air food festival that attracts locals and tourists alike. Every available space in town is taken up with a pasta stall, an ancient theatrical display, a musical event or a *degustazione* of local products. During the celebrations you can savour local specialties such as *n'dunderi* dumplings, and home-brewed liqueurs including the traditional *concerto* (made from richly flavoured and delicious hillside herbs from nearby Tramonti).

This festival is organised and overseen by the young and enthusiastic Andrea Reale, owner of the only four-star hotel in town, **Hotel Villa Romana**, where he and his chef offer week-long cooking courses throughout the year.

EATING AND DRINKING

I was once fortunate enough to watch chef Massimo Proto (right) prepare *n'dunderi* dumplings in the Ristorante L'Arsenale kitchen. He worked quickly and measured ingredients by instinct. He explained that the pasta must be made at the last minute, cooked immediately and eaten straight away, otherwise it turns to glug. A bowl of ricotta cheese squeezed through a potato ricer, good-quality Saracen flour, grated parmesan and a few egg yolks are all lightly worked together, rolled out and cut into small golf-ball-sized dumplings. He then rolled the dumplings and pressed them gently with a fork to create fine grooves to trap the sauce. He boiled the dumplings, deeming them ready when they rose to the surface, just like gnocchi. Meanwhile, over a very high flame, he quickly sautéed a handful of halved *piennolo* tomatoes with olive oil and salt. He then added the cooked dumplings to the tomatoes and tossed the pan over a decent flame, while adding a little more parmesan, some small cubes of fresh local provolone and a few scoops of the water the dumplings were cooked in. Five minutes of tossing and chatting later, and they were ready to eat.

Massimo recently traded his white t-shirt for a crisp chef's coat and hat at the impressive Torre Normanna in Maiori (see page 215).

TORTA DI RICOTTA E PERA
The mouthwatering ricotta and pear tart is another specialty of this food-driven town. For an impressive selection of these tarts, head for **Pasticceria De Riso**, right on the seafront.

BAR GAMBARDELLA

A Minorese friend recently introduced me to a little treasure of a bar tucked behind the lemon-coloured church of San Trofimena, **Bar Gambardella**. He swears they have the best coffee on the coast. He is not wrong, but my favourite thing about this place is the delicious homemade pastries (right). Their lime-coloured, lemon-flavoured chocolates are to-die-for, and their *delizia al limone* (lemon delicious) is one of the best I have tried. Gabriele Gambardella, the owner, told me they were the first to acquire a *limoncello* licence in the 1980s, when the home-brewed recipes went into commercial production. Gabriele's daughter Emiliana runs their *liquorificio* near the church, where they sell *limoncello* and other flavoured liqueurs – strawberry, blueberry, walnut, fennel and more. Francesco, his son, runs the pastry bar nearby.

JAZZ

It was not food, though, that brought me to Minori for the first time. My first experience of this town was during a visit to the wonderful mid-summer jazz festival. My darling guitar-playing friend from Positano, Fabrizio Canosa, introduced me to this fantastic event around 1995, when it first came to Minori. We would finish up work as quickly as possible in Positano, jump on our Vespas and zoom up the coast to arrive by 9.30 p.m., ready to enjoy the magnificent jazz artists who would flock to the coast from the Umbria Jazz Festival in the north. The musicians visit at staggered intervals throughout the busy summer months to perform under the stars, by the sea, or in a car park. The crowds are small, because that's all the town can handle, and if you are a jazz lover, these concerts are not to be missed. Check with the tourist information office in Minori for times and venues.

OVERLEAF: **Processional gowns are draped over the pews to dry inside the chapel of San Trofimena; a delicately embroidered** *morzetta* (cape) dating from the 1400s

SAN TROFIMENA

The legend of San Trofimena is much like that of the Madonnas of Positano and Maiori. A statue of this Sicilian martyr arrived by boat on the shores of Minori around 640 AD, and hence she became the patron saint of the town, and indeed the entire Amalfi Coast at the time (before Sant' Andrea of Amalfi arrived in the thirteenth century). But in Minori she is still celebrated no fewer than three times a year. On 5 November the *Minoresi* commemorate her martyrdom; on 13 July they remember the return of her remains from nearby Benevento in about 800 AD; and 27 November is the day they celebrate the rediscovery of her relic that disappeared in the late 1700s from its tomb. She is much loved, and a very busy saint!

While wandering around the backstreets, don't miss San Trofimena's twelfth-century basilica. It's a lemon-sherbet-coloured structure surrounded by pastel-pink and baby-blue houses. The crypt holds a beautiful period alabaster urn containing her remains.

VILLA ROMANA

Aside from the current dig in Positano, Minori possesses the clearest and best example of a Roman villa on the Amalfi Coast. The majestic seaside villa probably dates back to the Julio-Claudian era and boasts an extraordinary mosaic of a bull's head in the bathing area. Also on display are vases, vessels and coins from this era. The villa has not yet been entirely uncovered, and certain rooms still remain under the modern structures of the town. It is free to visit and a must-see.

LUNCHES

Lunch is the main meal of the day in the south of Italy. It's amusing to see the contrast between tourists and locals when it comes to dining out on the Amalfi Coast. You will often see tourists picking their way through a salad for lunch, then tucking into a huge plate of pasta, some dessert and buckets of wine for dinner, but the Italians tend to do it the other way round (so you can see why they need their siesta after lunch). Restaurants are often packed with tourists in the early evening, whereas the Italians will turn up as late as 10 p.m. (even with the kids in tow) and most likely nibble on something light. We all know which way of eating is better for us, so when in Rome…

Given the stellar coastal views and wide range of beachside restaurants here, you should always try to have lunch by the sea in summer when visiting the Amalfi Coast. For a delicious lunch, Italian-style, where you can happily wear your swimsuit, I can recommend:

Da Adolfo at Laurito Beach
Da Teresa in Vettica di Amalfi
Da Armandino, Il Pirata and La Gavitella in Praiano
La Tonnarella in Conca dei Marini

These other favourites are a little more up-market (you'll need to wear a bit more than just your swimsuit):

Ristorante A'Paranza in Atrani
Acqua Pazza in Cetara

A GUIDE TO FISH NAMES – TO HELP YOU ORDER

Many types of fish in Italy go by a different name in each region. For example, the sea bass is called *branzino* in the north, but on the Amalfi Coast and in neighbouring areas, it is know as *spigola*. To the right is a list of the types of fish you may spot on menus along the Amalfi Coast, and their name in English to help you identify them. *Pesce azzurro* (deep sea fish) from this region are particularly delicious, and include *riccola* (kingfish), *spada* (swordfish) and *tonno* (tuna).

NB: The letter 'L' (for *di levamento*) denotes that the fish is farmed (but don't worry – the seafood-loving chefs along the coast can make even a farmed fish taste wonderful). The letter 'I' (for *importato*) means that the fish has been imported.

aguglia	garfish
alici or acciughe	fresh anchovies
aringa	herring
bandiera	ribbon
cefalo	grey mullet
cernia	grouper
coccio or rondinella	rockfish
dentice	snapper (L)
grongo	conger
merluzzo	cod
orata	gilthead (L)
riccola	kingfish
rombo	a thicker version of sole
San Pietro	John dory (I)
sarago	bream (L)
scombro	mackerel
scorfano	scorpion or redfish
sogliola	sole (I)
spada	swordfish
spigola	sea bass (L)
tonno	tuna
triglia	red mullet

MAIORI, *IL PAESE DI SOLE E ARTE* (THE TOWN OF SUN AND ART) POPULATION: 6000 INHABITANTS: *Maioresi* ORIGINS OF THE NAME: Both Maiori and Minori were called Reghinna after the Etruscan leader who ruled these lands; Maiori eventually became Reghinna Major to differentiate it from Minori DISTRICTS: Erchie, San Pietro, Santa Maria delle Grazie, Vecite, Ponteprimario

PATRON SAINT: Madonna dell'Assunta, protector of anything and everything, celebrated on 15 August **MOTHER CHURCH** (*CHIESA MADRE*): Santa Maria a Mare **TOWERS:** Normanna, D'Erchie, Cesare, Badia, Lama del Cane, Capo Tummolo, to name a few **TYPICAL DISH:** *E' mulegnane c'a' ciucculata* (local dialect for eggplant with chocolate)

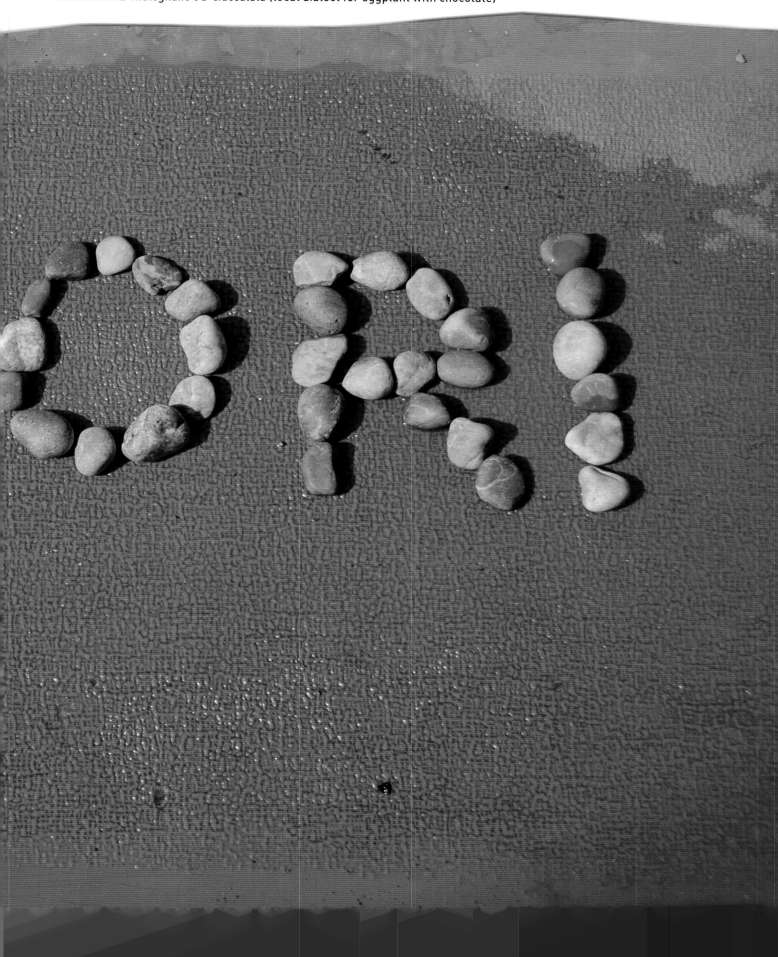

'I HAVE NEVER SEEN A MORE CHARMING PLACE...SO MUCH ROMANTIC SOLITUDE RESTORES ONE'S SOUL AND GIVES BIRTH TO A DESIRE TO LIVE THERE IN PEACE... OR AT LEAST SPEND A SUMMER.'

FERDINAND GREGOROVIUS. GERMAN HISTORIAN. ON ARRIVING IN MAIORI

VILLAGE OF TOWERS

Over the centuries Maiori has been invaded and conquered more often than any other coastal town, and every time another ruler took over, they seemed to build another monastery or tower. As a result, Maiori possesses more towers than any other town on the coast, and at one stage there were as many as five important monasteries here.

The biggest and most visible tower is the **Torre Normanna** (above right), today a restaurant. The **Torre d'Erchie** (below right), known as La Cerniola, was built by the Spanish in the 1500s and is regarded as one of the finest, not only for its structure, but also for its incredible position right on the delightful and enchanting beach of Erchie. La Cerniola is without a doubt the best-preserved tower on the coast and can be rented out for weddings, private parties and conferences.

Maiori has also had to battle with onslaughts from Mother Nature. It suffered two massive floods in 1910 and 1954, the latter almost completely destroying the central and northern part of town. Unfortunately there were few town-planning restrictions imposed after these disasters and Maiori was reconstructed with little regard for its previous structure.

However, there are many fascinating areas around the town that survived the floods. The backstreets possess the most delightful stairways, church façades and

tight narrow alleys. All reasons why Roberto Rossellini chose Maiori as a location for some of his great cinematic masterpieces during the 1940s and '50s, like *Paisà*, *Viaggio in Italia* and *Miracolo.* You can almost see Anna Magnani running barefoot down the steps as you wander through the little streets.

A TOWN OF CONTRASTS

Maiori has many beautiful old churches, grottos, and a castle and, rather oddly, many modern buildings as well. It's a bit like seven volumes of Harry Potter rolled into one!

As an important religious centre, Maiori received numerous privileges from kings and rulers over the centuries. There are plenty of rich and astounding churches to visit, which thankfully survived the floods. The most important church in Maiori is the beautiful Santa Maria a Mare with its typical Amalfi Coast dome in majolica green-and-yellow tiles. I call it the sister church of Positano – the resemblance is remarkable and they are frequently mixed up on postcard captions. Erected in the twelfth century and revamped in the 1800s, this sanctuary contains wonderful treasures in its crypt, including masterpieces from the 1600s by famous Maiori artists like Giovanangelo D'Amato.

Two beautiful grottos are accessible by boat: Grotta Sulfurea and Grotta Pandora. Grotta Sulfurea is known for its curative waters high in sulphur and magnesium. Grotta Pandora has an ethereal atmosphere, flooded in emerald-green light, and contains numerous stalagmites and stalactites.

Maiori even has its own castle, **San Nicola de Thoro-Plano** (below), that was really a ninth-century fortress and refuge originally used as a safe haven from invaders. It is privately owned today but can be visited by appointment. The views of the coast are spectacular from there, and well worth the hike up the hill.

PALAZZO MEZZACAPO AND THE HALL OF MIRRORS

One of the most outstanding and oldest antique structures right in the heart of town is the municipal council building. This elaborate 1800s structure was the Palazzo Mezzacapo, the private palace of the royal family, built by the Marquis Mezzacapo himself, who was also one of the Knights of Malta.

Il Salone degli Specchi (The Hall of Mirrors), on one of the top floors of the building, was the Marquis' favourite room and today is used for municipal meetings. It is a feast of elaborate gold trimmings and mirrors. The ornate frescoed ceiling depicts the Trionfo delgi Olimpici (The Triumph of the Olympiads) and watches over the administrators of today. The figures represent the four elements of nature: earth, wind, water and fire.

IL GRAND TURISTA

The 1800s and early 1900s was the era of the great intellectual traveller. Many international tourists made a 'grand tour' to this part of the world and settled in for months, painting their impressions of the beautiful coastline, studying its natural beauty, writing or composing music. The coast was full of artists, musicians, philosophers, architects and writers. And of course, many of these tourists stayed.

The 'painters of Maiori' were well known all over Europe at this time, not so much as a school of art but a way of painting. Some of the works can be seen today in the municipal council buildings of Minori, Ravello and Salerno.

BADIA DI SANTA MARIA DE OLEARIA

Just a few kilometres out of town is a treasure not to be missed. The Badia di Santa Maria de Olearia (right) was originally a Benedictine abbey and was later added to in the tenth century, then repeatedly in subsequent centuries. It houses three distinct chapels, stacked one on top of the other and etched out of a large roadside mountain grotto. The name of the abbey comes from the immense olive groves that reached as far down as the seaside. Check the opening hours from the tourist information office before you go.

SALT
Apart from possessing one of the main shipyards during the time of the Amalfi Republic, Maiori was important for its salt warehouses on its vast and open waterfront. During this period salt was considered very valuable, often taking the place of gold coins for payment in trade. So owning the salt warehouses was a bit like Maiori owning the bank!

Salt was often packaged for payment in soft leather pouches, with the amount only being determined correctly when the bag was placed on a table to observe how wide it spread. This is why it is considered bad luck to pass salt from hand to hand at the table today; in ancient times it was considered a dishonest offering of payment.

OPPOSITE: The elaborate interior and gardens of Palazzo Mezzacapo

MAIORI'S AMPHITHEATRE
Maiori boasts an enormous modern amphitheatre, right on the sea and surrounded by small fishing vessels. Seating up to 5000 people, this arena is the perfect venue for concerts and theatrical shows during the hot summer months.

ERCHIE BEACH
The beach of Erchie is another little pearl in the jewellery box of the Amalfi Coast. You can enjoy a wonderful summer's meal at **Delfino**, right on this delightful little beach, taking in the magnificent cinema-set view of sea, sun and tower.

LEGEND OF THE MADONNA STATUE

Maiori's patron saint is the Madonna, the busiest saint in Italy. According to legend, in 1204 a ship passing on its way to Constantinople took shelter just offshore from Maiori during a vicious storm. To lighten the ship's load a Byzantine cedar statue of the Madonna was thrown overboard. Later she was found washed up on the beach wrapped in cotton veils. Every 15 August the Madonna's faithful followers celebrate her arrival in this town with great gusto. Processions of villagers march the statue around the town, then a group of robust fishermen race up the sacred stairs to the church of Santa Maria a Mare, triumphantly holding their precious cargo at shoulder height.

EATING AND DRINKING

During a recent trip to Salerno, I stopped off in Maiori to eat at one of the few beachside restaurants that isn't completely dismantled during the winter months. A Maiorese friend had recommended **Nettuno**, right at the Cetara/Vietri end of the kilometre-long beach, and it was a wonderful surprise. I ate a generous grilled seafood platter full of scampi, *totani* and local *bandiera* fish (ribbon fish), as well as some delicious seafood gnocchi. And like most of the beach establishments along this stretch, Nettuno also has its own showers, change rooms, shaded areas, bar, beach brollies and beds – all terribly civilised!

The oldest restaurant in this village is **Mammato**, owned by Alfonso Mammato and established in 1873. The restaurant is decorated with beautiful ceramics and the seafood is exquisite. Like the surname Giordano in Tramonti, Mammato is *the* surname in Maiori, so when you meet a Mammato on the coast, you'll know instantly where they come from.

August is the month to savour the famous *e' mulegnane c'a' ciucculata* (eggplant with chocolate) in any of the top-quality patisseries or restaurants in Maiori. It's an unusual combination, but like strawberries with pepper and butter, it's a revelation. The eggplants are soaked in *concerto* and then dipped in chocolate.

A typical Maiorese pastry is the light-as-air *o suspire* (breath). It can be found at **Pasticceria Trieste**, which has been in business for more than fifty years and specialises in pastries made with almond paste. It's just up the road a bit from the Palazzo Mezzacapo.

FLOWERS AND TOWERS

At first sight, there appears to be only one type of flower on this coast: the bougainvillea. Its vivid shades cover almost every inch of the place – like the famous local lemon, *lo sfusato*, it adores the Amalfi Coast, and the feeling is mutual. When I lived there, I had an enormous terrace massed with bougainvillea, and we were best friends. I hated watering and had no idea about how to look after plants, but bougainvillea loves to be tortured – the less water I gave it, the happier it seemed to be.

Higher up in the Lattari Mountains, many varieties of wildflowers grow, and if we were having a special lunch or party at Da Adolfo's, I would pick the flowers growing in the woods on the pathway leading down to the restaurant. They would be propped up in glasses around the bar and tables, adding fragrance and colour to the occasion. You will also see little bunches of wildflowers framing many Madonna statuettes around the mountain pathways on the coast.

At funeral processions in Tramonti, it is a tradition to throw brightly coloured flowers in front of the hearse as it weaves its way up to the cemetery. These flowers become embedded into the asphalt and linger for days, like a wonderful mosaic in memory of the departed.

There are almost two dozen ancient towers majestically lining the Amalfi coastline. Some villages, like Furore, do not have one at all – others, like Maiori, have more than half a dozen. The majority of them were originally built in the Middle Ages to defend the townsfolk and their villages during the frequent violent invasions of the Maritime Republic. Today, they are often called Saracen towers, after the very people they were built to keep out. The majority of these towers have been restored or rebuilt many times over the years, and as a result reflect a variety of architectural styles.

Today, these towers serve various purposes. Some are in the hands of the local municipal councils and are used for exhibitions; some are restaurants or reception halls; and others are privately owned and often available to rent during the summer season. If you are thinking of staying in a tower, they are quiet, peaceful and very cool, though they can lack light due to their very small windows. Generous balconies are few and far between, but plenty of high look-out terraces afford spectacular sea views.

TRAMONTI, *LA CITTÀ DEL VINO* (THE CITY OF WINE) POPULATION: 4000 INHABITANTS: *Tramontini* or *Tramontani* ORIGINS OF THE NAME: Tramonti may derive from *tra i monte* (between the mountains), as that describes it perfectly – its lush land and hills are snuggled between the Lattari Mountains; another theory is that the name comes from *tramont ana*, the Arctic north wind that often blows in this area, or *tri ventium*, the turbulent meeting of three winds DISTRICTS: Polvica, Pucara, Ponte, Gete, Novella, Campinola,

Corsano, Capitignano, Pietre, Cesarano, Figlino, Paterno Sant'Arcangelo, Paterno Sant'Elia PATRON SAINT: Sant' Antonio di Padova, protector of lost objects, the hungry and the poor, celebrated on 13 June MOTHER CHURCH (*CHIESA MADRE*): San Bartolomeo – Novella TOWER: Torre Orsini TYPICAL DISHES: *Farro e fagoli* (spelt and beans) or *lasagna con funghi porcini* (lasagne with porcini mushrooms)

'A SHRED OF SWITZERLAND THAT SLIDES INTO THE AMALFI COAST. THIS IS WHAT I THOUGHT WHEN I DISCOVERED TRAMONTI, WITH ITS WOODS, ITS FLOWERS, ITS PEOPLE...'

LUCA GOLDONI, ITALIAN WRITER AND JOURNALIST

A UNION OF MOUNTAINOUS VILLAGES

This is the land of the farmer and the shepherd. There is none of the traffic that sometimes plagues the coast – just rich green pastures and abundant woods.

Sometime between 500 and 550 AD the Romans settled Tramonti, using timber from the surrounding forests to construct their housing. The wood was also used centuries later for shipbuilding, and is still a major commodity today.

Tramonti covers a huge spread of rich mountainous land nestled in the heart of the Lattari Mountains. It is the largest commune on the Amalfi Coast – approximately 24 square kilometres – and is made up of 13 districts. Each district has its own church (some have two), spanning medieval times right through to the modern day. Because the town is so spread out and hilly, it is best to visit by car – you can rent one just down the road in Maiori.

This area is the principal source of produce for the entire Amalfi Coast, such as lemons, chestnuts, meat, milk and vegetables. The townspeople also produce beautiful cheeses, oils, wines and liqueurs, as well as the baskets to put them in. When dining out in Positano, we would never refuse when a restaurateur announced, 'And tonight's special is sausages from Tramonti' or 'Some wonderful goat's cheese from Tramonti has just arrived'. It was always a mark of the exceptional quality and freshness of the produce.

HOW THE FIRST
PIZZAS WERE MADE

The first pizzas of Tramonti were made using a biscuit/bread dough, dressed with lard, tomato, olive oil, garlic and oregano. If the family was wealthy, a few *alici* (anchovies) were tossed on top too. Mozzarella was not used at all, and the pizza was cooked in the oven together with the daily bread. Today this style of pizza is eaten every year during All Saints Weekend. In ancient times, it was a way of showing respect for the dead. When a family was in mourning they would not eat meat or cook at home, hence the traditional pizza was eaten, and as people left the cemetery they would purchase a slice from the *contadini* (country farmers).

PIZZA

History tells us that pizza was born in Naples with the classic Margherita, named after Queen Margherita of Savoia, which explains the patriotic colours: red tomato, green basil and white mozzarella. However, there are a lot of coastal folk, including gastronomic historian Ezio Falcone, who disagree that a Neapolitan produced the first pizza, insisting that the first pizza-maker originally came to Naples from Tramonti and brought his own mozzarella with him. This area of the Amalfi Coast is known all over Italy for producing the best pizza-makers in the country.

Unfortunately for coastal residents, about 3500 pizza-makers have migrated to the north of Italy or to other countries to practise their art. But you can still eat a delicious pizza in Tramonti. My favourite pizzeria is **Montagne Verde Da Mario** in Cesarano, right on the crossroads for Ravello. Their wood-fired oven burns year-round and their wines are all local. Located in the fresh air of the mountains, this retreat is warm and cosy in winter, and cool and inviting in summer. Vincenzo (right) and his dad, Mario, have been running this pizzeria for over forty years, so they certainly know what they are doing when it comes to pizza.

FOOD FESTIVALS

There are a healthy number of food festivals in Tramonti. Culture and folklore always accompany the best food festivals in this area and most of the action takes place in the piazza or on the streets, so you can't miss it.

- The Wine and Food Festival runs from 10 September–1 October and is held in the district of Cesarano.

- The Chestnut Festival (Castagne) starts at the end of September and goes through most of October. Its events take place mostly on the weekends, and some are also held in Cesarano.

- The Wine Harvest Festival is held in early October, when you can visit the cellars and vineyards in the area of Campinola. A similar wine festival is celebrated from 10–11 August in Gete.

- The Pizza Festival runs from 12–13 August in Pietre.

ABOVE: Maria Profeta sells her zucchini flowers from her roadside stall

EATING AND DRINKING

The jovial Luigi Reale (left) runs **Osteria Reale** in Gete, and his restaurant and cellars are open all year round. Be sure to try one of his delicious *mare/monte* (sea/mountain) pastas, such as *broccoletti e vongole* (broccoli and clams). Luigi not only serves fantastic food but also produces approximately 12 000 bottles of wine a year from locally grown grapes, including Cardamone, which is pressed from 200-year-old vines. The shady terraced restaurant is surrounded by many of his vineyards and is situated just around the corner from the wonderful ruins of the Cappella Rupestre (Rocky Chapel), which was severely damaged during the floods of 1735. If you would like to visit the chapel, just ask Luigi to point you in the right direction. But if you want to stick around, he can also sort you out with a room for the night.

For a deluxe meal you cannot beat **Cucina Antichi Sapori** at Campinola. Owners Giuseppe and Antonietta ran a noted restaurant in the north of Italy, specialising in southern flavours, but they have returned to Antonietta's hometown of Tramonti. This unexpected and classy little restaurant may seem a bit out of place in its rustic surroundings, but I can guarantee you will not be disappointed.

WINE

Tramonti grows a different grape for every district in the town – thirteen varieties in all – and over the years Tramonti has been home to many talented winemakers.

Back in 1977, Giuseppe, owner of **Apicella Wines**, produced about 3000 bottles of Tramonti Rosso a year from less than a hectare of land. Today his grandchildren, Prisco and Fiorina, run the business with the same passion, but produce closer to 60 000 bottles from about seven hectares of land. Prisco likes to think big, he tells me, as he rests on one of his 2000-litre French oak vats. And he only uses vats this size 'because bigger vats wouldn't fit through the door!' Scippata is their big reserve red – a super Tramontino wine. Look for the Costa d'Amalfi Tramonti wine label and you are in for a treat.

Another excellent drop is produced at **San Francesco di Chiara Di Palma** in Corsano. This new winery produces an excellent white that is hard to beat with a seafood lunch, the Tramonti Bianco 2005 Costa d'Amalfi.

TRAMONTI *CARTIERA*

L'Antica Cartiera Amalfitana is one of the two remaining paper factories on the Amalfi Coast (the other is Amatruda of Amalfi). Dario Cavaliere has run this factory for over eighteen years and was delighted to show me around when I visited. The factory is tucked below the road on the left as you head up the mountain in the village of Pucara. I drove past the steep driveway several times before I worked out where it was, so I hope their signage improves! The building has recently been restored, in keeping with its 1700s origins. It is wonderful to see the room (left) where the paper was hung to dry, with its long, rough poles slotted into large holes in the wall that allow the air to circulate freely.

I watched Raffaele Giordano (right) mix fibres of American and Colombian birch, poppy and conifer in a large vat of milky, smelly mush, and then produce before my eyes a sheet of beautifully embossed paper on a small netted frame. *Miracolo*!

CONCERTO

Tramonti produces every liqueur imaginable, but the local delicacy is the aromatic *cuncierto* (pronounced kun-chi-er-toe), today known as *concerto*.

As *limoncello* is to Amalfi, so *concerto* is to Tramonti – it's *the* mountain dew. This ancient mix of barley, aromatic herbs, and spring water from the mountains has been around for centuries. It was invented by the nuns of the Conservatorio di San Giuseppe e Teresa from Pucara, who established this institute in the early 1700s to educate the noble daughters of the region. These nuns were also the founders of the *melanzana dolce*, the sweetened eggplant forerunner of Maiori's famous *e' mulegnane c'a' ciucculata*. I like to drink *concerto* chilled – sacrilege if you are drinking it as a digestive, but so good in the middle of summer.

To purchase a bottle of *concerto* you can go to the **Tentazioni** store, which is a street hut practically in the middle of the road as you climb up to Tramonti from Maiori in the village of Pucara. Surrounded by their lemon groves, Peppe and Maria Giulia Giordano can supply you with a good selection of the delicacies of this town – from various liqueurs to home-baked bread and wonderful handmade cheeses. And if you need a pick-me-up, Peppe will make you an espresso on the run.

If you are looking for a beautiful bottle to do justice to this delicious brew, head to **Badia**, at the top of town in Cesarano, just in the piazza near the bell tower. Emilio Giordano (yes, everyone in Tramonti seems to have this surname) also makes an excellent *sfusatello* (a variant on *limoncello* made with the best *sfusato* lemons of the area). It is a pretty little shop and Emilio is also a font of historical information on the area if you are interested.

FARM-STAYS

For a simple and relaxing visit to Tramonti, try *agriturismo* (farm-stays). These offer visitors a taste of simple home living on a working farm and good wholesome food from the garden. There are quite a few farm-stays available in Tramonti, such as **Il Raduno** and **Il Frescale**. But if you want a *real* hotel, head to the top of the mountain to **Il Cupido**.

CHEESE

The population of Cesarano is made up chiefly of goats and sheep, whose milk yields some of the finest and most delicious raw-milk cheeses on the coast. **Riccardo Giordano** (who appears on the cover of *The Food and Wine Guide to Naples and Campania* by Carla Capalbo) is a shepherd for the new millennium. He produces the best sheep- and goat's-milk cheeses for taste and quality.

For wonderful mozzarella, head to **Caseificio di Vicedomini Mansi Caterina** in Cesarano. It's a bit of a challenge finding the production area, as there is no signage – you just have to ask around. The one tonne of local milk used by this cheese-maker every day produces some of the coast's best fresh and smoked mozzarella, known as *fior di latte* (flower of the milk). They also produce ricotta, bocconcini, provolone and *caciotta* (a type of ricotta, and my favourite). Caterina Mansi (far right) supplies many of the local restaurants.

The excellent **Antica Latteria di Tramonti** in Gete sells many of the dairy products produced by local *caseifici*, and is a wonderful store.

BASKET WEAVERS

Basket weaving is sadly a diminishing craft in Tramonti, but the area is nonetheless renowned for its weavers, who make robust baskets woven with large flat-shaved strips of chestnut bark. Thanks to the abundant local chestnut trees, these solid baskets of Tramonti have been produced for centuries. I had Tramonti baskets scattered through my house for the eighteen years I lived on the coast, containing everything from firewood to my son's shoes, books, lemons and tools. And I have seen labourers transport rocks inside them – they are virtually indestructible.

There are few weavers left in Tramonti today, but whenever there is a town fair, you will also see a basket stall or two. The remaining weavers all work from home. Luigi and Rosa Amodio Amarante (near right) produced such thick and strong baskets that you couldn't believe that Luigi made them by hand. The baskets were immaculate. Similar ones can be found all over Campania but they are not as precise or well made as those from Tramonti.

LEMONS

The iconic lemon that grows along the Amalfi Coast is known in local dialect as *lo sfusato*, from the Italian *affusolato*, meaning tapered or elongated. Its shape makes it easy to distinguish from the many other types of lemons grown in this area. *Lo sfusato* is also renowned for its small nipple at one end, rough, warty skin, thick pith, abundant juice, delicate flavour, bright yellow hue, lack of pips and, most of all, its unmistakably clean, strong aroma. And in addition to all this, recent studies have shown that the Amalfi Coast lemon has twice as much Vitamin C as any other lemon on the planet. *Lo sfusato* is the lemon from heaven!

It is believed the first lemons were brought to this area in Roman times, possibly transported here via trade with Arab countries. The Amalfi Coast once produced about 8 per cent of the nation's lemons, but in recent times has been overtaken by Sicily – but only in terms of quantity, not quality. In 2001, *lo sfusato* was awarded the prestigious European IGP (Protected Geographical Indication) recognition, and it is now known worldwide as Il Limone Costa D'Amalfi. This status is awarded to agricultural produce that rely on their natural habitat to achieve certain outstanding characteristics. To maintain this standard, *lo sfusato* must be grown and picked according to certain strict requirements, and the local growers drape the lemon trees in black netting for most of winter to protect them from harsh weather conditions. It's hard work being a protected lemon today!

The lemon is renowned for its medicinal properties, and was being used as far back as the Middle Ages to ease gastrointestinal infections and protect against scurvy. And the people of the Amalfi Coast still swear by *lo sfusato* as a curative. Sergio's dad, Adolfo, would recommend a glass of lemon juice (the juice of at least four lemons, with no water or sugar added) to ease an upset stomach, nausea, hangovers, vomiting or all of the above – it is a shock while you are drinking it, but it works every time. He would also suggest squeezing the juice of half a lemon into a short black espresso (with no sugar or milk) to relieve headaches, a remedy that also works brilliantly. I would sometimes place a slice of cool lemon on Marco's forehead and secure it loosely with a bandage when he had a slight fever. It was refreshing and definitely helped alleviate his temperature.

The lemon plays a role in almost every part of day-to-day life in this region. In fact, most houses have a beautiful lemon tree outside the front door, not just for good luck but as a necessary part of life. Apart from cooking, here's a few of the other million and one uses for *lo sfusato*:

- A teaspoon of raw sugar mixed with the juice of half a lemon is a great exfoliant. Rub it all over your hands – they will be smooth as a baby's bottom. My girlfriends and I would include this in our home beauty treatments. Try it on your face as well, but don't rub too hard!

- You can use lemon juice to clean almost everything in the kitchen – pots, pans, kitchen surfaces, the fridge, the sink – and after handling fish or berries, use lemon juice to clean your hands.

- Adolfo would rub some lemon juice, mixed with a little olive oil, into his scalp every day to cleanse and soften the rough, dry skin. Also great for elbows, heels and knees.

- After long, boozy dinner parties, I would burn some lemon peel in a burner or metal dish to revitalise the smoky room.

LIMONCELLO

The sweetness and delicate flavour of
lo sfusato makes the best *limoncello* in existence.
Here is Adolfo's brother's recipe:

rind of 5 lemons (sliced as close to the pith as possible)
300 ml pure alcohol (good luck finding this quantity at
a decent price outside of Italy, though!)
250 g sugar
300 ml just-boiled water

Soak the lemon rind in the alcohol for 2–4 weeks.
Dissolve the sugar in the just-boiled water and allow
to cool. Remove the rind from the alcohol and mix
the remaining liquid with the dissolved sugar. Strain
through a fine sieve and drink, preferably in small,
chilled glasses, taking small sips (and try to stop after
two glasses).

TARA, *IL PAESE DELLA COLATURA DI ALICI* (THE TOWN OF ANCHOVY SYRUP) POPULATION: 2400 INHABITANTS *Cetaresi* GINS OF THE NAME: There are many theories but my favourite is that the name derives from the Latin word *cetus*, the name of legendary whale that beached itself in this area DISTRICT: Fuenti

PATRON SAINT: San Pietro, protector of fishermen, celebrated on 29 June **MOTHER CHURCH** (*CHIESA MADRE*): San Pietro
TOWER: Torre Vicereale di Cetara **TYPICAL DISH:** *Linguini alla colatura di alici* (linguine with anchovy syrup)

'CETARA, A GENTLE INLET OF THE COAST, WHERE MAN NEVER FORGETS THAT THE SEA OFTEN GIVES BUT SOMETIMES TAKES MORE THAN IT HAS GIVEN.'

SECONDO SQUIZZATO, THE MAYOR OF CETARA

THE PEARL OF THE AMALFI COAST

If Atrani is the diamond in this jewellery-box coastline, then Cetara is definitely the pearl. Life in this pretty, pocket-sized village is all about what comes out of the sea – commercial fishing for tuna and anchovies being the villagers' livelihood for centuries. The oversized fishing vessels bobbing gently in the tiny port appear to be bigger than the town itself. Cetara is situated in a deep valley at the base of Mount Falerio and if you happen to blink while driving through, you may miss it. So take your time and turn off to discover this enchanting little gem.

I have a special fondness for Cetara. My favourite Italian actor, the comedian Toto, shot one of his first films here, *L'uomo, la Bestia e la Virtu (The Man, the Beast and the Virtue)*. He managed to make me laugh even when I first arrived in Italy and didn't speak a word of Italian – a true genius.

FISHING

This sleepy fishing village has endured its fair share of invasions, hardship and turmoil over the centuries. It was the first town to be ransacked by the Saracen pirates in 879, and in the 1500s it was devastated by an army from Sicily raised by an Islamic convert, with many of its inhabitants taken into slavery or massacred. After this tragic era the Torre Vicereale was erected as a lookout to protect this vulnerable hamlet from invaders. Today the tower (now a private home) is *the* symbol of Cetara. And no matter how hard people try to commercialise this small

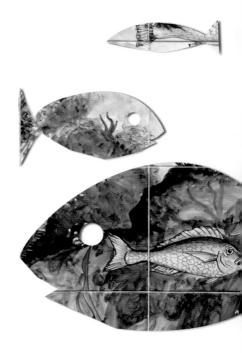

fishing port, the *Cetaresi* just won't be part of it. Fishing, and only fishing, has always been their livelihood; they have little interest in developed tourism.

Wander down to the port and you will see the brightly coloured tuna trawlers that keep this village alive. Their fleet of vessels was once the largest and most productive in Italy and the Cetara fishing industry was renowned all over Europe. Today Cetara continues to sell tuna all over the world but mostly to the Japanese, who prize the dark tasty meat fished in these waters.

FISHY SPECIALTIES

If you love eating fish, then you must try Cetara tuna. Preserved in a jar with olive oil, it is unlike any canned variety you have ever tasted. (All good Italian tuna is usually sold in a jar, not a can.) Ninetta, my next-door neighbour in Positano and a brilliant dressmaker, would often give me a jar of tuna she had made for her husband's fish shop while fitting me for a new skirt. It was the best I've ever had.

The other local specialty not to be missed is the famous *colatura di alici* (anchovy syrup), a precious by-product from the process of salting *alici* (anchovies). The *alici* mature under layers of salt in large vats from May to November. The vats are closed and weighted down with heavy rocks to squeeze the soul out of the anchovies, then just before Christmas a hole is made in the bottom of the barrel – and voila! – you have this incredibly aromatic golden juice to enhance your dishes. Decades ago, locals would produce their own *colatura* and give it away as a generous Christmas gift. In poorer times this wonderful tasty liquid took the place of the more expensive olive oil as a condiment to have with pasta. You can use *colatura* wherever you would normally use salt, but use only a drop at a time as it's very strong. Amalfi Coast locals generally use it to enhance fish dishes, whether they be stews, pastas or risottos. Today you can purchase *colatura* all year round. And don't forget the fresh *alici* themselves, my favourite Amalfi Coast fish delicacy. Fried, stuffed, baked, grilled, chopped over pasta, marinated with lemon juice and vinegar – however you serve them, they are a real local treat.

COLATURA DI ALICI
To purchase *colatura di alici* or other delicious fishy goods, head down to **Delfino** or **Cetarii** on the port.

PERNOD FOR THE *CETARESI*
If you wander into a bar in Cetara, don't be surprised to see the locals drinking the French aperitif Pernod, a popular tipple in this town. The drink was brought here many years ago by visiting French fishing fleets. Cetara has taken the southern seaside French town of Sète as their twin city, where today thousands of *Cetaresi* reside and work in the fishing industry.

ANCHOVY PERFUME, ANYONE?
Until only a few years ago, Cetara was famous for the *puzza di alici* (strong anchovy smell) around town. Today, thankfully, the smell is gone, but the pride in the *alici* remains.

FISHY FESTIVALS

If you are in the area at the end of July or the beginning of August, don't miss the celebration of A Tutto Tonno (All About Tuna) in Cetara. At night the entire beach area turns into a huge open-air restaurant, and it's all about tuna! You can try it grilled, fried, stewed, baked – however you like it. And as you would expect, this delicious food is accompanied by lively traditional music and performances.

For the anchovy celebrations you will have to come back in December for Antichi Sapori (Antique Flavours), where new recipes and methods of using the famous Cetara *colatura di alici*, and other typical products of Cetara, are shared. The excellent local restaurants also get involved, preparing exclusive recipes based on the *colatura di alici*.

Cetara's patron saint, San Pietro, is, naturally, the protector of all fishermen, and he is celebrated on 29 June in an explosion of colourful fireworks. The saint's bust is carried procession-like on a boat-shaped platform around the town, eventually arriving at the port, where he is met by a flurry of local fishing boats, trawlers, dinghies, row boats – basically anything that floats. This, to me, is one of the prettiest saint's day processions on the coast.

SAN PIETRO

The main church of San Pietro (right) combines ninth-century foundations with ornate baroque embellishments, a classic Amalfi Coast majolica dome and a medieval bell tower. It has recently been given a facelift with beautiful new bronze doors (left). Constructed in 2005, they depict sculpted scenes of San Pietro and his brother Sant' Andrea proudly holding two beautiful fish.

EATING AND DRINKING

Close to San Pietro is the church of San Francesco, built in the 1500s, which is attached to the old convent of the same name. Today the cloisters are a restaurant called **Al Convento**. You can enjoy local food while admiring the seventeenth-century frescos that were barely saved from enthusiastic renovators a few decades ago.

Almost next door is **Ristorante San Pietro**. They do a terrific mixed antipasto, and excellent *alici fritti* – fried anchovies served in a rough paper cone to absorb the excess oil. Francesco, the owner, once explained to me that before the war this was how everything – from flour to cooked food – was packaged at the local store. Francesco also prepares a magic *zuppa di farro* (spelt soup) with fresh anchovies, flavoured with oregano and *colatura di alici*. He explained that oregano is one of the herbs that goes particularly well with this magic liquid.

Nestled into the humble port area of town and just down the path from the large fishing trawlers is a very special eatery, **Acqua Pazza**, owned by the two Gennaros. Gennaro I (below right) nurtures guests with detailed explanations of each dish and possesses a thorough knowledge of the restaurant's extensive wine list, while Gennaro II is tucked away in the kitchen, creating innovative and wonderful food. Antipasti delights I have enjoyed here include shaved octopus tentacles on a bed of lightly dressed salad, sea snails poached in a tomato sauce, and whole grilled baby octopus on a bed of potato purée. And to follow, an *assaggio* (taste) of pasta dishes: spaghetti with *colatura di alici* and *paccheri* (short pasta) with tuna roe and zucchini. Out of this world! Everything is cutting edge in this place – from Gennaro I's 'skater boy' haircut right down to their provocative business card, designed by well-known Vietri artist Ugo Marano and featuring a sketch of an elongated fish's nose that becomes a male's penis (a play on words – *pesce* means fish in Italian and penis in Italian slang). The two Gennaros don't do anything by halves.

BOATS

Boats are integral to life on the Amalfi Coast – you won't get very far without them. They can be your own personal limo, taxi, dining room, entertainment area, and sometimes even your bedroom! For those who live here, having a boat (even just a dinghy) is just as important as having a roof over your head.

If you are visiting for a short time, one of the best ways to see the coast is to hire your own little *gozzo* (small wooden boat) from one of the boat hire groups on the main beach of any beach-access town: **Lucibello**, **Blue Star** or the Esposito brothers at **Cassiopea**. You can cruise up and down the coast for the day, with or without your own boat boy, stopping in one of the many beach restaurants for lunch on the way, or you can take the ferry or a fast hydrofoil to Amalfi, Capri, Sorrento or Naples. This is the way to go in summer – no traffic, no curves, no searing hot roads; just sheer pleasure.

A boating day trip with Salvatore and Gennaro Capraro of **L'uomo e il Mare** is a must. These two have been commercial fishermen all their lives. You will often see Salvatore on the main quay in the early morning, weaving a wheelbarrow full of freshly caught fish between the queues of people waiting for the hydrofoil. After hours at sea he'll make a dash for home up the staircase near the jetty, shower, change, then return to start up one of his big comfy tour boats, and head off minutes later with a load of happy daytrippers. They do tours to the Galli Islands, Capri and Amalfi, setting out in the morning and having lunch at one of the delicious coastal restaurants, like my favourite, **Da Teresa** in Amalfi. Salvatore will often take his own super-fresh catch along to the restaurant and have them fry it up for lunch. There are plenty of opportunities to swim along the way, even under magnificent waterfalls. Weather permitting, cheeky Salvatore will often squeeze the tour boat into the tiny, narrow Fiord di Furore for a party teaser!

Salvatore and Gennaro offer night fishing tours as well, usually for *totani* (flying squid) if the moon is not too full and bright. Fishing for *totani* is a great night out, and was how I spent my first date at sea with Sergio. In anticipation of our flying squid dinner, we nibbled on bread and cheese and drank wine while dipping our lines in and out of the water till we felt a distinct tug, the signal of a bite. Then we would reel the squid in, swiftly and smoothly; quite an art when you are dealing with an energetic little sea creature. A bright light hung over the side of the boat not only attracts the squid to the bait, it also allows you to see the squid when it's a few metres from the surface – and this is when you need to take cover, as the squid will spray angry squirts of sea water all over you as it emerges. If the *totani* are asleep, it can be a pretty dull night of fishing, but if they are biting it is one of the most exciting experiences you will have!

If you simply want a day on a boat on the dazzling blue waters of the Mediterranean, **Raimondo**'s pretty little *gozzo* is perfect. It holds up to six people, and has a spacious sunbaking area with soft pillows, and shade if required. On request you can enjoy *caponata* salad and chilled wine for lunch. Raimondo himself is priceless – a fabulous diver (very handy if the anchor gets stuck), a wonderful chef and a most knowledgeable guide.

VIETRI, *IL PAESE DELLA CERAMICA* (THE TOWN OF CERAMICS) POPULATION: 8600 INHABITANTS: *Vietresi* ORIGINS OF THE NAME: During Roman times it was known as Veteri (from the latin *vetus* meaning old city) – it is thought the Romans discovered ancient ruins in the town DISTRICTS: Marina, Molina, Raito, Albori, Benincasa, Dragonea PATRON SAINT: San Giovanni Battista, protector

VIETRI, *IL PAESE DELLA CERAMICA* (THE TOWN OF CERAMICS) POPULATION: 8600 INHABITANTS: *Vietresi* ORIGINS OF THE NAME: During Roman times it was known as Veteri (from the latin *vetus* meaning old city) – it is thought the Romans discovered ancient ruins in the town DISTRICTS: Marina, Molina, Raito, Albori, Benincasa, Dragonea PATRON SAINT: San Giovanni Battista, protector of monks, celebrated on 24 June **MOTHER CHURCH** (*CHIESA MADRE*)**:** San Giovanni Battista **TOWERS:** Torre d'Albori, Torre di Vito Bianchi, Torre Crestarella **TYPICAL DISH:** *I piscetielli* (meaning 'little fish' in the local dialect), handmade short pasta topped with seafood and *piennolo* tomatoes

'WHEN SPRING COMES, VIETRI AT SEVEN IN THE MORNING APPEARS AS A BEAUTIFUL YOUNG GIRL, AWAKENING AT FIRST LIGHT, WARMLY ANNOUNCING ITS READINESS TO GLOW.'

GIGI AMATURO. ITALIAN WRITER

IT'S ALL ABOUT CERAMICS

Some historians dispute whether Vietri sul Mare is actually part of the Amalfi Coast – but for me, it definitely is. It offers the same great food, the same neat beaches, the same dialect and the same pasta with *vongole* as the other towns. And all those ceramics you can purchase from Positano to Cetara? They all originated in Vietri.

This is the furthest town from Positano on the Amalfi Coast, and the hardest to reach both because of sheer distance and the sometimes heavy traffic. But whenever friends or family visited me in Positano, Vietri was a must for a side trip, and they would always buy up big on ceramics, from chic mono-coloured bowls to naïve multi-coloured animals created back in the early 1900s. The choice of ceramics is almost embarrassing, and at the largest factory or the smallest boutique the staff always offer to wrap, pack and ship the goods – every shopper's dream when buying a heavy or bulky item while on holiday.

Today nearly everyone in this town is involved in ceramics somehow. In the last few decades practically every shop façade has been decorated with ceramics, and there are countless ceramics showrooms. Accommodating this riot of colour is an architecture with distinct baroque and rococo flavours, as evidenced by the striking church of San Giovanni Battista (left). This church was originally founded in the tenth century on the highest point of the old town and has undergone numerous changes over the centuries. If you get lost wandering around the back alleys of Vietri, just look up, and the magnificent majolica dome of San Giovanni Battista and its extended bell tower will lead you back to the heart of the old town.

THE BEGINNINGS OF AN INDUSTRY

Vietri has been involved one way or another with ceramics since the Middle Ages. Located between Salerno and Amalfi, Vietri benefited from the connections these two great trading towns forged with the Orient, and their ceramic designs were influenced by Byzantine and Greek motifs. By the eighteenth century, more than fifty kilns worked around the clock in Vietri. In the twentieth century the *Vietresi* continued tirelessly to reproduce their crockery and geometric tiles in the classic 'Greek' or 'sponge' style using basic tones of green.

When World War II began, many free-thinking German artists arrived in Vietri, seeking refuge. The 'German period' that followed was the most productive and creative era in the history of ceramics in Vietri. Finding sanctuary here, the Germans developed the artisan trade and turned it into an industry, producing marketable objects of beauty, and made Vietri ceramics what they are today.

Many famous craftspeople made this little town their home, such as Polish-born Irene Kowaliska, who created the naïve and child-like images still seen on plates all over the world today. She also developed her wonderful fabric designs while residing on the Amalfi Coast. The German ceramicist Richard Doelker created the famous *ciucciariello* (green donkey, left), the symbol of Vietri ceramics recognised worldwide. Many more Europeans in this era also left their mark.

Examples of these wonderful ancient pieces (right) can be found just up the hill in the ceramics museum inside the tower Belvedere of Villa Guariglia in Raito.

CERAMICHE SARA

An old friend of mine, Elio Rispoli, married a beautiful young woman from Vietri some years ago. Sara is the daughter of Assunta and Osvaldo of **Ceramiche Sara**, located just at the entrance to Vietri on the Amalfi Coast road, and I have come to know them and their work well over the years.

In Osvaldo's younger days he was an award-winning *vasaio*, or master potter. He showed me photographs of his winning entries at the famous potters competition in Fienza, where entrants would attempt to shape the largest platter possible on a wheel without the platter collapsing. Osvaldo won this competition two years running back in the 1970s. There was a lot of muscle and sweat involved! He told me the enormous platters were then used to dry tomatoes.

Ceramiche Sara has come a long way since Osvaldo's pottery days. They have recently finished an entire floor in a private villa in Valencia, Spain, for a wealthy Milanese businessman.

ABOVE: A ceramic relief embedded into the wall at Ceramiche Sara

PINTO

Ceramica Pinto have been in business since way back in 1625 and the name is now synonymous with beautiful, hand-thrown tiles. Vincenzo Pinto, who ran the business in the early 1900s, presided over a period of extraordinary creativity that coincided with the influx of German artisans. Today the business is run by Vincenzo's children and grandchildren, who continue the Pinto tradition of producing their famous hand-crafted 'Vietri White' tiles (right). They are known for their enamels, which are bright and durable, and they are the only remaining production house to use the original antique stone windmills to crush the sand.

Although Pinto produces all types of ceramics, it is most famous for its tiles with wonderful geometric patterns. You will see these tiles in churches, private villas, hotels, royal palaces and restaurants all over Italy, not just on the Amalfi Coast. Don't miss the showroom – on the outside there is the most beautiful and simple tiled wall (left) displaying everyday scenes with characteristic Pinto wit, in shades of eggplant and white.

SOLIMENE

Vietri ceramicist Vincenzo Solimene's family has been producing ceramics for over one hundred years and has gained an international reputation for its work. The Solimene factory, retail outlet, creative studio and laboratory are all housed inside one of Vietri's most spectacular examples of modern-day architecture, **Ceramica Artistica Solimene** (right and below). In the early 1950s Vincenzo Solimene met Torino-born architect Paulo Soleri, who had been an apprentice of Frank Lloyd Wright in America, and shared his dream of creating an amazing factory for his works of art. The dream became a reality when in 1954 the Ceramica Artistica Solimene was built, under the talented and watchful eye of the architect. This landmark building has more than 200 000 hand-thrown ceramics embedded into its façade. Today the Solimene factory is run by Vincenzo's daughter, Giovanna, a passionate businesswoman who offers courses for young ceramicists wanting to perfect their talents.

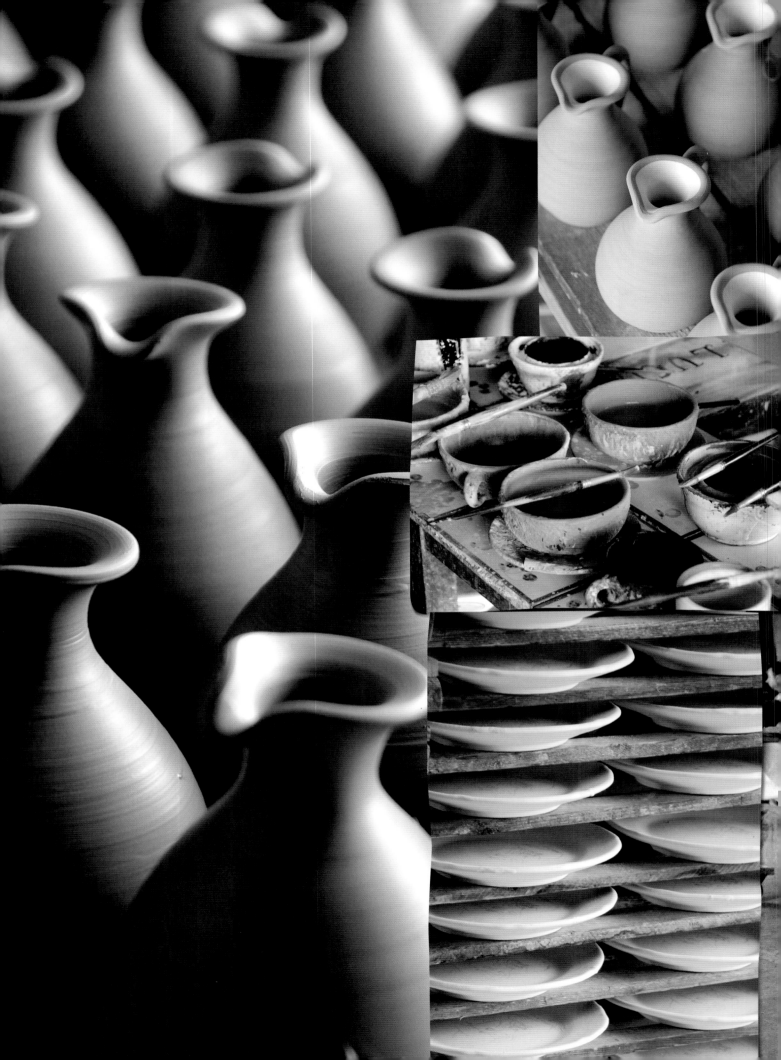

UGO MARANO

My favourite Vietri artist was Ugo Marano (pictured), a great individualist and creative soul, who created ceramic vases up to three metres tall. Like his vases, Ugo himself was tall, thin, beautiful and extremely original. The long and lonely hours spent working on his sculptures only made him a more sociable and adorable person when in company.

I first heard about Ugo Marano while living in Positano. There was to be a sort of 'artistic happening' on the main beach in the middle of summer, at which this great artist from Vietri would perform his *ballo sui bicchieri*, the dance on the glasses. We all gathered near the Buca di Bacco on the main beach at sunset and as the ethereal music built slowly, this tall, slim Poseidon-like man emerged from the sea, stripped to a loincloth, with eyes of Mediterranean-blue. Before him, on the small square between the restaurants, were a thousand upturned terracotta mugs (a Vietri version of glasses). While we gazed on and the hypnotic music played, he stood on the mugs and danced with feather-like delicacy. It was an Ugo sensation! A true free spirit; there is nothing ordinary about Ugo.

He was asked to design one of his signature ceramic sculptures for the Torino Winter Olympics in 2006, and was the sole artistic creator/director of the famous 50-hectare Parco Dora in Torino (once part of the Fiat factory in the 1980s).

ENZO SANTORIELLO

Ceramicist and kiln-maker Enzo Santoriello of **Ceramica D'Arte Santoriello** recently bought an old glass factory in Vietri that resembles an aeroplane hangar in proportions, and is big enough to accommodate his massive ovens. Without Enzo, Ugo would have had trouble firing his three-metre-tall vases in one piece. Enzo specialises in constructing tailor-made kilns for unique works of art. But he has bigger plans for this space than simply building giant ovens. It will also be a meeting place for artists and sculptors from all over the world to gather, discuss, eat and drink, create, ponder and generally just hang out – a modern-day artists' atelier.

RAITO

Recently a new five-star hotel has popped up *in collina* (on the hillside) in the beautiful old medieval area of Raito. It's called **Hotel Raito**, and is all pools, palms and peace, overlooking Vietri and its neighbouring towns. This very special little village also houses the famous Museo della Ceramica in the Villa Guariglia, where King Vittorio Emanuele III would take his vacations, and where today you can enjoy summer concerts.

THE LEGEND OF THE DUE FRATELLI (THE TWO BROTHERS)

The two famous rocks that rest off the main beach of Vietri have a tale to tell. According to locals, many years ago two brothers brought their sheep down from the mountains one day to the beach of Vietri to wash their fleeces. While sitting on the beach they noticed a beautiful young woman lying on a rock at the water's edge. So enchanted by her beauty were they, that they did not notice a storm sweeping in. When it struck, the young woman was washed off the rock and out to sea. Without thinking, the two brothers plunged in to try to save her, and naturally their sheep followed. Unfortunately neither shepherd nor their flock had much knowledge of swimming, and all drowned. The young woman was the daughter of the king of the sea, the great Poseidon, who was so moved by the plight of these poor shepherds that he placed two large rocks just off the shores of Vietri in memory of their courage.

ALBORI

For a really quiet 'meditation in the vegetation', the district of Albori, with its tiny dollhouse buildings attached to one another, is the epitome of peace. It has an enchanting sixteenth-century church, Santa Margherita di Antiochia, which appears suspended on this mountain 300 metres above the sea. The precious ceramics inside are not to be missed.

A great plate of *pasta penne alla cuppitiello* (short pasta with seasoned local vegetables) at the **Ristorante Garden**, with its jaw-dropping view over Vietri, makes a perfect lunch.

EATING AND DRINKING

If you are a seaside lover then Marina di Vietri, below the main part of town, is the spot for some great food and a swim. The best swimming spot is Ciurma, right in front of the Due Fratelli (The Two Brothers) rocks. **La Ciurma** is a great place for daytime beach snacks, and becomes a romantic destination for a candlelit dinner later in the day. They serve all the simple summer favourites like *pasta con le vongole*.

When I last visited Enzo Santoriello he took me next door to **Bar Russo** for the best *baba'*, a typical Neapolitan dessert of sponge cake soaked in rum. And as a refresher, we drank thick myrtle berry juice. Right near the main crossroad in Vietri, this is a good spot for a breather if your ceramic purchases are weighing you down.

Just up on the corner, **Vera Cucina** has a terrace overlooking the busy ceramic strip of Vietri. They serve a great *pasta con troffietti vongole e porcini* (pasta with clams and porcini mushrooms), and their seafood pasta is also excellent and worth trying, particularly in a town known for its fantastic array of seafood. This is the best pit-stop for lunch if you are on a ceramics shopping spree.

Down in the beach area, you simply must have a gelato at the biggest, most modern gelato shop I have ever seen – **Bar Gelateria Eco del Mare**. It seats over 200 people (in high season) and, as you can imagine, the gelato is terrific.

MOZZARELLA

In my early days in Positano, Sergio's dad, Adolfo, would take the whole family out to the ancient Greek city of Paestum, which has the best-preserved Greek temples in the world outside of Athens. But instead of marvelling at the ancient ruins, we would all be set to work picking the *mirto* berries that grew amongst them, from which Adolfo would concoct his own homemade liqueur. The area's famous buffalo mozzarella was another reason for these day trips (Adolfo *loved* his mozzarella). The rich and fertile soil of the former swamplands around Paestum is perfect for buffaloes, and the area is famous for the production of buffalo-milk products.

Tenuta Vannulo is a local dairy farm renowned for its delicious organic dairy products, including yoghurts and ice cream. The property has been in Antonio Palmeiri's family since the early 1900s, and when he took it over a couple of decades ago, he had a definite goal in mind: to turn this working farm into a paradise of artisan organic buffalo-milk products. Everything from classic bocconcini made from fresh buffalo milk to delicious flavoured yoghurts, buffalo-milk butter, fluffy ricotta and lashings of gelato are available from the farm (but you have to be quick if you want mozzarella – it usually sells out by noon). People come from as far away as Milan, lining up for their cheeses, before bolting back to Naples airport just in time to catch their flight home.

Vannulo do not supply restaurants, hotels or even the corner deli. They sell only to the general public – a kilo here, a kilo there, and you must go to the farm to purchase from the tiny store there. The milk is unpasteurised and all products are made by hand (no machinery is used at all). They have 600 head of buffalo and they only use the milk produced by their own stock, which is why produce is sometimes limited, but believe me, these girls give up their milk happily! On a recent warm summer's day when I visited Vannulo I saw some buffaloes standing lazily under light sprinklers having a shower, while others stood side by side under the massage machine. They are treated with homeopathic remedies, and glass pots containing an organic liquid hang around the property, attracting and killing the flies (there's not a fly in sight – it's buffalo heaven!). Every morning at 4 a.m., the milk is transported across a manicured driveway into the mozzarella-making rooms, where it is churned, pulled, twisted, and squeezed (the verb *mozzare* means to cut off, twist, or squeeze). A few hours later, a huge stainless steel vat of beautifully prepared mozzarella bobbing in water is wheeled out to the little shop, where throngs of anxious buyers await.

Tenuta Vannulo is a two-hour drive from Positano, and the Greek temples of Paestum are just minutes away. It makes for a great day trip.

RESOURCES

POSITANO

Tourist information
Via del Saracino, 4, Positano
Tel: +39 089 875067
www.aziendaturismopositano.it

3 Denari (shoes)
Via del Saracino, 8/10, Positano
Tel: +39 089 875062

Antica Sartoria (boutique)
Via Piazza dei Mulini and main beach
Tel: +39 089 811754
anticasartoria@tiscali.it

Bagni d'Arienzo (restaurant)
Via Arienzo, 16, Positano
Tel: +39 089 812002

Bar Bruno
Via C. Colombo, 83, Positano
Tel: +39 089 875392

Bar Internazionale
Via G. Marconi, 306, Positano
Tel: +39 089 875434

Blue Star (boat hire)
Via G. Marconi, 82, Positano
Tel: +39 089 811888
www.bluestarpositano.it

Buca di Bacco Bar and
La Pergola Restaurant
Via del Brigantino, 35/37, Positano
Tel: +39 089 811461
www.bucapositano.it

Cassiopea (boat hire)
Tel: +39 089 8123484
www.cassiopea-positano.com

Ceramica Assunta (ceramics)
Via C. Colombo, 97, Positano
Tel: +39 089 875008
www.ceramicassunta.it

Ciro's (fruit and veg)
Via G. Marconi, 188, Positano
Tel: +39 089 812169

Conca del Sogno (restaurant)
Via S. Marciano, 9, Nerano
Tel: +39 081 8081036
www.concadelsogno.it

Covo dei Saraceni (hotel)
Via Regina Giovanna, 5, Positano
Tel: +39 089 875 400
www.covodeisaraceni.it

Cuomo (butcher)
Via Mulini, Positano
Tel: +39 089 875422

Da Adolfo's (restaurant)
Via Laurito, 40, Positano
Tel: +39 089 875022
www.daadolfo.com

Da Ferdinando (bar)
Spiaggia di Fornillo, Positano
Tel: +39 089 875365
www.casaceleste.net/stabilimento.htm

Donna Rosa (restaurant)
Via Montepertuso, 97/99, Positano
Tel: +39 089 811806
www.donnarosapositano.it

Emporio Sirenuse (boutique)
Via C. Colombo, 103, Positano
Tel: +39 089 811468

Franchino's (street hamburger van)
A'Garritta area, Positano

Grassi (bar)
Via Fornillo, Positano
Tel: +39 089 811620

Hotel Palazzo Murat
Via Mulini, 23, Positano
Tel: +39 089 875177
www.palazzomurat.it

Hotel Poseidon
Via Pasitea, 148, Positano
Tel: +39 089 811111
www.hotelposeidonpositano.it

Il Capitano (bric-a-brac,
owner Luigi Cafiero)
Via C. Colombo, 171, Positano
Tel: +39 081 5322151

Il Fornillo (restaurant)
Via Pasitea, 266, Positano
Tel: +39 089 811954

Il Grottino Azzurro (restaurant)
Via G. Marconi, 158, Positano
Tel: +39 089 875466

Il Ritrovo (restaurant)
Via Montepertuso, 77, Positano
Tel: +39 089 812005
www.ilritrovo.com

Il San Pietro (hotel)
Via Laurito, 2, Positano
Tel: +39 089 875455
www.ilsanpietro.it

La Bottega di Brunella (boutique)
Via Pasitea, 72, Positano
Tel: +39 089 875228
www.brunella.it

La Cambusa (restaurant)
Piazza A. Vespucci, Positano
Tel: +39 089 875432
www.lacambusapositano.com

La Marinella (bar)
Via Positanesi D'America, 42, Positano
Tel: + 39 089 811843

La Zagara (bar)
Via Dei Mulini, 8, Positano
Tel: +39 089 8122892

Le Sirenuse (hotel)
Via C. Colombo, 30, Positano
Tel: +39 089 875066
www.sirenuse.it

Lucibello (boat hire)
Via del Brigantino, 9, Positano
Tel: +39 089 875032
www.lucibello.it

L'uomo e il Mare (boat trips)
Tel: +39 089 811613
www.gennaroesalvatore.it

Moda Positano (shoes)
Via del Saraceno, 30, Positano
Tel: +39 089 875656
www.modapositanosandali.it

Music on the Rocks/Le Terrazze
(disco/restaurant)
Via Grotte dell'Incanto, 51, Positano
Tel: +39 089 875874
www.musicontherocks.it
www.leterrazzerestaurant.it

Next 2 (restaurant/bar)
Via Pasitea, 242, Positano
Tel: +39 089 8123516
www.next2.it

Pepito's (boutique)
Via Pasitea, 39, Positano
Tel: +39 089 875446
www.pepitos-fashion.com

Pescheria Pasquale De Lucia
(fish shop)
Via G. Marconi, 392, Positano
Tel: +39 089 811301

Pupetto (hotel and bar)
Via Fornillo, 37, Positano
Tel: +39 089 875087
www.hotelpupetto.it

Raimondo (boat trips)
Tel: +39 089 811751
Mob: +39 339 2110733

Ristorante il Cantuccio
Marina del Cantone, Nerano
Tel: +39 081 8081288
www.ristorantecantuccio.com

Ristorante Maria Grazia
Marina del Cantone, 65, Nerano
Tel: +39 081 8081011

Safari (shoes)
Via della Tartana, 2, Positano
Tel: +39 089 811440
www.safaripositano.com

Santa Croce (restaurant)
Via Nocelle, 19, Nocelle
Tel: +39 089 811260

Saraceno d'Oro (restaurant)
Via Pasitea, 254, Positano
Tel: +39 089 812050

Sirocco's Macelleria (butcher)
Via G. Marconi, 332, Positano
Tel: +39 089 811527

Taverna del Capitano (restaurant)
Piazza delle Sirene 10/11,
Marina del Cantone, Nerano
Tel: +39 081 8081028
www.tavernadelcapitano.it

Taverna del Leone (restaurant)
Via Laurito, 43/45, Positano
Tel: +39 089 875474

Tre Sorelle (restaurant)
Via Marina, 5, Positano
Tel: +39 089 811922

PRAIANO

Tourist information
Via G. Capriglione, 116B, Praiano
Tel: +39 089 874557
www.praiano.org

Africana Night Club
Via Torre a Mare, 2, Praiano
Tel: +39 089 874042
www.africananightclub.it

Bar Mare
Via Marina di Praia, 7, Praiano
Tel: +39 089 874326

Bar del Sole
Via G. Capriglione, 120, Praiano
Tel: +39 089 813079

Casa Angelina (hotel)
Via G. Capriglione, 147, Praiano
Tel: +39 089 8131333
www.casangelina.com

Centro Sub (scuba diving centre)
Via La Praia, Praiano
Tel: +39 089 812148
www.centrosub.it

Ceramica Liz Art (ceramics)
Via Roma, 42, Praiano
Tel: +39 089 874307
www.lizartceramiche.com

Da Armandino (restaurant)
Via Marina di Praia, 1, Praiano
Tel: +39 089 874087
www.trattoriadaarmandino.it

Frank Carpegna (adventure walks)
Tel: +39 329 6422637
www.positanowalkingadventures.com
ringhio51@hotmail.com

Hotel Bar Le Fioriere
info@lefioriere.it
www.lefioriere.it

Il Pirata (restaurant)
Via Terramare
Tel: +39 089 874377

La Brace (restaurant)
Via G. Capriglione, Praiano
Tel: +39 089 874226

La Fioriere (hotel/bar)
Via Nazionale, 138, Praiano
Tel: +39 089 874203

La Gavitella (restaurant)
Via Gavitella, 1, Praiano
Tel: +39 089 8131319
www.lagavitella.it

Maurizio de Rosa (adventure walks)
Tel: +39 339 1718194
Tel: +39 340 3675642
www.sulsentierodeglidei.it

One Fire (bar)
Gavitella Bay, Praiano
Tel: +39 338 3508555

Paolo Sandulli (artist)
Mob: +39 339 4401008
p.sandulli@alice.it

Pasquale and Marina Aiello
(healer & masseuse)
Tel: +39 089 874136
Mob (Marina): +39 339 5966300

Pasquale Scala (guitar-maker)
Via Umberto I, 68a, Praiano
Tel: +39 089 874894
www.liuteriascala.com

Re Jewels (jeweller)
Via G. Capriglione, 129, Praiano
Tel: +39 089 874812
www.rejewels.it

Tramonto D'Oro (hotel)
Via G. Capriglione, 119, Praiano
Tel: +39 089 874955
www.tramontodoro.it

Tritone Hotel
Via Campo, 5, Praiano
Tel: +39 089 874333
www.tritone.it

Tutto per Tutti (delicatessen)
Via Umberto I, 30, Praiano
Tel: +39 089 874016
www.marinotuttopertutti.it

FURORE

Tourist information
Via Mola, 29, Furore
Tel: +39 089 874100
www.comune.furore.sa.it

Al Monazeno (restaurant)
Via Anna Magnani, Furore
Tel: +39 349 0772544
www.monazeno-fiordo-furore.com

Bacco Hotel and Restaurant
Via G.B. Lama, 9, Furore
Tel: +39 089 830360
www.baccofurore.it

Furore Inn Resort
Via dell'Amore, 1, Furore
Tel: +39 089 8304711
www.furoreinn.it

Marisa Cuomo Wines
Via G.B. Lama, 14, Furore
Tel: +39 089 830348
www.granfuror.it

CONCA

Tourist information
Via Roma, Conca dei Marini
Tel: +39 089 831301
www.concadeimarini.org

Da Claudio Bed and Breakfast
Via Smeraldo, 67, Conca dei Marini
Tel: +39 089 831621
www.euroconca.it

Ippocampo (restaurant)
Via Marina, 43, Conca dei Marini
Tel: +39 089 831153

La Tonnarella (restaurant)
Via Marina, 1, Conca dei Marini
Tel: +39 089 831939
www.ristorantelatonnarella.it

Polisportiva (restaurant *Le Bontà de Capo* and sports centre)
Via I Maggio, 14, Conca Dei Marini
Tel: +39 089 831515
www.amalficoast-restaurant.com

Ristorante Risorgimento
Via Marina, 42, Conca dei Marini
Tel: +39 089 831897

Sabatino Laudano (videographer)
Tel: +39 089 831750
info@cvconca.com

AMALFI

Tourist information
Via delle Repubbliche
Marinare, 27, Amalfi
Tel: +39 089 871107
www.amalfitouristoffice.it

Amatruda (paper-makers, wholesale only)
Via delle Cartiere, 100, Amalfi
Tel: +39 089 871315
www.amatruda.it

Bar Francese
Piazza Duomo, 20, Amalfi
Tel: +39 089 871049

Da Teresa (restaurant)
Spiaggia Santa Croce, Amalfi
Tel: +39 089 831237
www.dateresa.it

Hotel Centrale
Largo Duchi Piccolomini, 1, Amalfi
Tel: +39 089 872608
www.amalfihotelcentrale.it

Hotel La Conchiglia
Piazzale dei Protontini, 9, Amalfi
Tel: +39 089 871856
www.amalfihotelconchiglia.it

Hotel Santa Caterina
Via S. Quasimodo, Amalfi
Tel: +39 089 871012
www.hotelsantacaterina.it

Il Ninfeo (for access to Villa Romana)
Via Lorenzo d'Amalfi, 28, Amalfi
Tel: +39 089 8736353
www.amalficoastceramics.com

La Caravella (restaurant)
Via M. Camera, 12, Amalfi
Tel: +39 089 871029

Marina Grande (restaurant)
Corso delle Repubbliche
Marinare, 4, Amalfi
Tel: +39 089 871129

Museo della Carta (paper mill museum)
Via delle Cartiere, 24, Amalfi
Tel: +39 089 8304561
www.museodellacarta.it

Pasticceria Pansa
Piazza Duomo, 40, Amalfi
Tel: +39 089 871065
www.pasticceriapansa.it

Ristorante Pesce d'Oro
Via G. Augustariccio, 561, Amalfi
Tel: +39 089 831231

Ristorante Zaccaria
Via C. Colombo, 9, Amalfi
Tel: +39 089 871807

Stella Maris (restaurant)
Viale della Regione, 2, Amalfi
Tel: +39 089 872463
www.stella-maris.it

ATRANI

Tourist information
Piazza Umberto I, 1, Atrani
Tel: +39 089 872479

A'Scalinatella (hostel)
Piazza Umberto I, 5/6, Atrani
Tel: +39 089 871492
www.hostelscalinatella.com

Bar Birecto
Piazza Umberto I, Atrani
Tel: +39 089 871017

La Risacca (bar)
Piazza Umberto I, 16, Atrani
Tel: +39 089 872866
www.risacca.com

L'Argine Fiorito (bed and breakfast)
Via dei Dogi, 45, Atrani
Tel: +39 089 8736309
www.larginefiorito.com

Ristorante A'Paranza
Via Dragone, 1, Atrani
Tel: +39 089 871840
max70@tiscali.it

Ristorante Zaccaria
(see Amalfi)

RAVELLO

Tourist information
Via Roma, 18, Ravello
Tel: +39 089 857096
www.ravellotime.it

Bric-a-Brac
Piazza Duomo, 4, Ravello
Tel: +39 089 857153

Caffè Calce (bar)
Via Roma, 2, Ravello
Tel: + 39 089 857152

The Cameo Factory
Piazza Duomo, 9, Ravello
Tel: +39 089 857461
www.museodelcorallo.com

Cumpà Cosimo (restaurant)
Via Roma, 44/46, Ravello
Tel: +39 089 857156

Hotel Caruso
Piazza San Giovanni
del Toro, 2, Ravello
Tel: +39 089 858801
www.hotelcaruso.com

Hotel Palumbo
Via San Giovanni
del Toro, 16, Ravello
Tel: +39 089 857244
www.hotelpalumbo.it

La Rondinaia (hotel)
Tel: +39 089 858370
www.villarondinaia.it

Palazzo Sasso (hotel)
Via San Giovanni
del Toro, 28, Ravello
Tel: +39 089 818181
www.palazzosasso.com

Villa Cimbrone
Via S.Chiara, 26, Ravello
Tel: +39 089 857459
www.villacimbrone.com

Villa Eva (wedding venue)
Via S.Chiara, 3, Ravello
Tel: +39 089 857255
www.villa-eva.it

Villa Maria
Via S.Chiara, 2, Ravello
Tel: +39 089 857255
www.villamaria.it

Villa Rufolo
Piazza Duomo, Ravello
Tel: +39 089 857621

SCALA

Tourist information
Piazza Municipio, 1, Scala
Tel: +39 089 857 115
www.comune.scala.sa.it

Da Lorenzo (restaurant)
Via Frate Gerardo Sasso,
10, Scala
Tel: +39 089 858290

Latteria Santa Caterina
(dairy products)
Via G. Mansi, 9, Scala
Tel: +39 089 857655

Oreste Bottiglieri
(adventure consultant)
Tel: +39 339 2830261

Trattoria Antico Borgo
(restaurant)
Via Noce, 4, Scala
Tel: +39 089 871469

Zi'Ntonio (restaurant)
Via Torricella, 39, Scala
Tel: +39 089 857118

MINORI

Tourist information
Via Roma, 30, Minori
Tel: +39 089 877087
www.proloco.minori.sa.it

Bar Gambardella and Liquorificio
Corso Vittorio Emanuele, 37, Minori
Tel: +39 089 877299
www.gambardella.it

Hotel Villa Romana
Corso Vittorio Emanuele, 90, Minori
Tel: +39 089 877237
www.hotelvillaromana.it

Il Pastaio (handmade pasta)
Tel: +39 089 853706

Pasticceria De Riso
Piazza Cantilena, 28, Minori
Tel: +39 089 853618
www.deriso.it

MAIORI

Tourist information
Corso Reginna, 73, Maiori
Tel: +39 089 877452
www.aziendaturismo-maiori.it

Delfino (restaurant)
Via Torre di Cesare, Erchie, Maiori
Tel: +39 089 855063

Mammato (restaurant)
Via Lungomare Amendola, Maiori
Tel: +39 089 877036

Nettuno (restaurant)
Via Lungomare G. Capone, Maiori
Tel: +39 089 877594

Pasticceria Trieste
Corso Reginna, 112, Maiori
Tel: +39 089 853575

Pasticceria Vittoria
Via Lungomare Amendola,
26/27, Maiori
Tel: +39 089 877743

San Nicola de Thoro-Plano
(castle)
Tel: +39 338 9403552
(Signor Crescenzo De Martino)

Torre d'Erchie (tower)
Tel: +39 340 4730988
www.lacerniola.it

Torre Normanna (tower restaurant)
Via Diego Tajani, 4, Maiori
Tel: +39 089 877100
www.torrenormanna.net

TRAMONTI

Tourist information
Piazza Treviso, Polvica, Tramonti
Tel: + 39 089 856811
www.comunetramonti.it

Antica Latteria di Tramonti
(dairy products)
Localita Fornovecchio,
Gete, Tramonti
Tel: +39 089 876920

Apicella Wines
Via Castello S.Maria, 1, Tramonti
Tel: +39 089 856209
www.giuseppeapicella.it

Badia (liquor shop)
Piazza Cesarano, 42, Tramonti
Tel: +39 089 855344
www.illimoncello.com

Caseificio di Vicedomini
Mansi Caterina (dairy products)
Via C. Di Lieto, 28, Tramonti
Tel: +39 089 876985
luvrus@hotmail.com

Cucina Antichi Sapori (restaurant)
Via Chiunzi, 72,
Campinola, Tramonti
Tel: +39 089 876491
www.tramontipizza.
org/pizzerie/antichisapori

Il Cupido
Via Chiunzi, 93, Tramonti
Tel: +39 089 876974
www.cupidohotel.it

Il Frescale (farm-stay)
Via Fiscale, Figline, Tramonti
Tel: +39 089 876317
info@ilfrescale.it

Il Raduno (farm-stay)
Via De Matteis, 11, Tramonti
Tel: +39 089 856102
www.ilraduno.it

L'Antica Cartiera Amalfitana
(paper-makers)
Via Nuova Chiuzi, 14, Tramonti
Tel: +39 089 855432
lacasrl@infinito.it

Montagne Verde Da Mario
(restaurant)
Via Cesarano, Tramonti
Tel: +39 089 855338

Osteria Reale (restaurant)
Via Cardamone, 75, Tramonti
Tel: +39 089 856144
info@osteriareale.it

Riccardo Giordano
(cheese-maker)
Via Foria, Cesarano, Tramonti
Tel: +39 089 855332

San Francesco di Chiara
Di Palma (winery)
Via Solficiano, 18, Tramonti
Tel: +39 089 876748
aziendasanfrancesco@libero.it

Tentazioni (liquor shop)
Via Santa Croce, 4, Tramonti
Tel: +39 089 855401
www.liquoritentazioni.it

CETARA

Tourist information
Piazza S. Francesco, Cetara
Tel: +39 089 261593
info@prolococetara.it

Acquapazza (restaurant)
Corso Garibaldi, 38, Cetara
Tel: +39 089 261606
www.acquapazza.it

Al Convento (restaurant)
Piazza San Francesco, 16, Cetara
Tel: +39 089 261039
www.alconvento.net

Cetarii (fish products)
Via Largo Marina, 48/50, Cetara
Tel: +39 089 261863
www.cetarii.it

Delfino (fish products)
Sapori Cetaresi, Corso Garibaldi,
44, Cetara
Tel: +39 089 262010
www.delfinobattistasrl.it

Ristorante San Pietro
Piazza San Francesco, 2, Cetara
Tel: +39 089 261091
www.sanpietroristorante.it

VIETRI

Tourist information
Via O. Costabile, 4, Vietri sul Mare
Tel: +39 346 39569757
www.prolocovietrisulmare.it

Bar Gelateria Eco del Mare
Via Giuseppe Pellegrino, 128, Marina
(frazione di Vietri Sul Mare)
Tel: +39 089 210323
info@ecodelmare.info.it

RESOURCES

Café Pasticceria Russo
Corso Umberto I, 168, Vietri
Sul Mare
Tel: +39 089 761030
www.cafepasticceriarusso.it

Ceramica Artistica Solimene
(ceramics)
Via Madonna degli Angeli, 7,
Vietri Sul Mare
Tel: +39 089 210243
www.solimene.com

Ceramica Pinto (ceramics)
Corso Umberto I, 31, Vietri Sul Mare
Tel: +39 089 210271
www.pintoceramica.it

Ceramica D'Arte Santoriello
(ceramics)
Via Nuova Raito, 18, Raito (frazione
di Vietri Sul Mare)
Tel: +39 089 210912
Santoriello.vincenzo@tiscalinet.it

Ceramiche Sara (ceramics)
Via Costiera Amalfitana, 14/16,
Vietri Sul Mare
Tel: +39 089 210053

Hotel Raito
Via Nuova Raito, 9, Raito (frazione
di Vietri Sul Mare)
Tel: +39 089 7634111
www.hotelraito.it

La Ciurma (restaurant)
(open during summer only)
Via Cristoforo Colombo, Marina
(frazione di Vietri Sule Mare)
Tel: +39 089 761194

Ristorante Garden
Via Comunale, 7, Albori (frazione di
Vietri Sul Mare)
Tel: +39 089 212572

Tenuta Vannulo (dairy products)
Via G. Galilei, 10, Capaccio Scalo
Tel: +39 828 724765
www.vannulo.it

Vera Cucina (restaurant)
Corso Umberto I, 156, Vietri Sul Mare
Tel: +39 089 761868

BIBLIOGRAPHY

Campania, Incisivo, Electa Napoli – ATI Publicis, Salerno, Italia, 2005.

Capalbo, Carla, *The Food and Wine Guide to Naples and Campania* (1st edition), Pallas Athene Ltd, London, 2005.

D'Episcopo, Francesco and Masullo, Tonino, *Vietri sul Mare*, Tipolitografia LITA snc, Vietri sul Mare, Italia, 1996.

Gargano, Olimpia, *Amalfi la citta' famosa, la citta' da scoprire*, Tipolitografia Somma, Castellammare di Stabia, Italia, 1995.

Gho, Paola (curator), *Osterie D'Italia Sussidiario del mangiarebere all 'italiana 2007*, Slow Food Editore, Rotolito Lombarda Piotella, Italia, 2006.

Gruppo di Azione Locale, *Costa d'Amalfi*, Costiera Amalfitana Monti Lattari, Grafiche Ponticelli S.p.A. Castrocielo, Italia, 2001.

Itinerari, Costa d'Amalfi e Penisola Sorrentina, Grafiche Lama, Italia, 2002.

Russo, Flavio, *Le Torri Vicereali Anticorsare della Costa d'Amalfi*, Tipolitografia G. Dolgetta, Sarno, Italia, 2002.

Scala, Giovanni, *I Sentieri Sacri*, Praiano e Vettica Maggiore, De Luca Editore, Salerno, Italia, 2001.

Ulisse Di Palma, Salvatore, *Ricordi di Ravello*, Gutenberg Lancusi, Italia, 2000.

WEBSITES

www.costiera-amalfitana.com
www.ecostieramalfitana.it/costieraamalfitanatour/tourcost.htm
www.giracostiera.com
www.positanonews.it
www.santiebeati.it

All information provided is correct at time of printing.

INDEX

INDEX

ACKNOWLEDGEMENTS

Many people have given me the strength firstly to tackle, then complete, this exciting project. Without them, it would have remained one of those dreams never to be realised.

My son Marco's quiet, calm manner (obviously not inherited from me!) has helped me enormously over the last few years and made it possible for me to even consider such a huge undertaking as writing this book.

My mother, Maggie, has provided incredible emotional support, often believing in me more than I did. Her considerable patience and wise advice (especially insisting I always 'keep my voice') have been invaluable.

I thank all the Italian saints that my darling stepbrother Nico Prossimo is so well-read, and fluent in both Italian and English. He has enthusiastically assisted me with the translations, including the quotations.

Thanks to my darling sister Brooke, for offering to feed and support me if I went broke during the process of this project! Thankfully I didn't have to call on her, but knowing the support was there was so comforting. And *grazie mille* to Daniele Bella for so generously sharing all his native *Positanese* knowledge with me, and allowing me to publish his delicious family recipes that have been part of my life for the past twenty years.

With all my heart, I thank my darling mate and passionate photographer Carla Coulson, who first sowed the seed of writing a book about the Amalfi Coast when we met all those years ago, and then almost killed herself shooting this book in just three weeks! What a magnificent job she has done.

A huge thanks to Patricia Schultz for all the generous and valuable advice she's shared with me, gained over decades of experience in travel writing. Despite the usual hiccups along the way, she managed to keep me on track and always laughing with her priceless sense of humour.

Thanks to my publisher, Julie Gibbs and Ingrid Ohlsson for giving me the chance to make it all happen, and the talented staff at Penguin, especially my editor Virginia Birch and designer Daniel New, for endless hours spent calmly sorting through hundreds of photos and basically putting up with me! Many thanks also to Evi O. for her clever illustrations and freelance graphics guru Grahame Smith for his wonderful eye and concept development.

And how lucky I was to have found such a great Italian contact in the travel world here in Australia, Antonio Bamonte of Viatour, who booked all my research trips to Italy. He is also the official representative in Australia for the region of Campania, and provided me with valuable contacts at the Provincia di Salerno, most notably its president, Angelo Villani.

Of all the wonderful journeys I have taken in my life, writing this book has been by far the most challenging and rewarding. It would have been so easy to do whilst I was living in Italy but, as with most projects I've tackled in my life,

I chose the more complicated path! Bringing together such a wealth of information would have been impossible without the help and support of so many old and new friends on the Amalfi Coast – you all made a hard job so much easier: Benedetta Russo of the Municipality Tourist Council in Positano, for her hundreds of emails and research assistance; Constantino Mandara (Positano), for all his wonderful insights on religious matters; Gaetano Marrone (Positano), for sharing his expertise on the food and wines of this region; Rosalba Irace, of the Tourist Information Office in Praiano, for her hundreds of informative emails; Giovanni Scala (Praiano), for his wealth of historical knowledge; Raffaele Ferraioli, mayor of Furore and developer of the town's profile as *il paese che non c'e*; Gaetano Milo (Conca dei Marini), President of the Festival Committee of San' Antonio; Pino Milo, Technical Officer of the Municipality of Conca dei Marini; Pino Cobalto (Amalfi), for sharing his library and extensive knowledge of towers with me; Ezio Falcone (Amalfi), for his colourful advice on historical gastronomy on the Amalfi Coast; Michele Buonocore, traffic policeman and calligraphist, for sharing his passion of Atrani; Gabriele Mansi, Scala's mayor, for taking me on a wonderful tour of the town's magnificent churches; Luigi Schiavo of the Municipality Tourist Council of Ravello; Eugenia Apicella of the Communita' Montana, for answering my thousands of emails on Scala and Ravello so promptly; Andrea Reale, owner of the hotel Villa Romana in Minori, for being the first person to enthusiastically embrace me in his wonderful town; Enzo Mammato, traffic policeman, for sharing his historical expertise on his beloved Maiori; Lucia Mammato, of the Municipality Tourist Council in Maiori; Carmen Imparato, of the Municipality Tourist Council in Tramonti, for her help in pointing me in the right direction every time; Secondo Squizzato, the mayor of Cetara, for his quote and his insights into this tiny village; Tiziana del Sio and Vittoria Sciavone, of the Municipality Tourist Council in Vietri, for supplying all the valuable information I requested; and finally, a big thank you to the dozens of other Amalfi Coast natives who have helped me along the way, enabling me to fulfil the dream of telling my story.

LANTERN

Published by the Penguin Group
Penguin Group (Australia)
250 Camberwell Road, Camberwell, Victoria 3124, Australia
(a division of Pearson Australia Group Pty Ltd)
Penguin Group (USA) Inc.
375 Hudson Street, New York, New York 10014, USA
Penguin Group (Canada)
90 Eglinton Avenue East, Suite 700, Toronto, Canada ON M4P 2Y3
(a division of Pearson Penguin Canada Inc.)
Penguin Books Ltd
80 Strand, London WC2R 0RL England
Penguin Ireland
25 St Stephen's Green, Dublin 2, Ireland
(a division of Penguin Books Ltd)
Penguin Books India Pvt Ltd
11 Community Centre, Panchsheel Park, New Delhi – 110 017, India
Penguin Group (NZ)
67 Apollo Drive, Rosedale, North Shore 0632, New Zealand
(a division of Pearson New Zealand Ltd)
Penguin Books (South Africa) (Pty) Ltd
24 Sturdee Avenue, Rosebank, Johannesburg 2196, South Africa

Penguin Books Ltd, Registered Offices: 80 Strand, London, WC2R 0RL, England

First published by Penguin Group (Australia), 2008

10 9 8 7 6 5 4 3 2

Text copyright © Amanda Tabberer 2008
Photography copyright © Carla Coulson 2008

The moral right of the author has been asserted

All rights reserved. Without limiting the rights under copyright reserved above, no part of this
publication may be reproduced, stored in or introduced into a retrieval system, or transmitted, in
any form or by any means (electronic, mechanical, photocopying, recording or otherwise), without
the prior written permission of both the copyright owner and the above publisher of this book.

Design by Daniel New © Penguin Group (Australia)
Cover design by Ricardo Felipe and Daniel New © Penguin Group (Australia)
Initial design concepts by Grahame Smith
Illustrations by Evi O.
Cover and internal photography by Carla Coulson
Family snaps in the introduction and on pages 62, 88–91, 106, 144–147, 184, 208–211, 266–269 courtesy Amanda Tabberer;
photograph on page 12 (main b&w) courtesy Nicolas Potts; photographs on page 88 (top left), page 90 (centre right), page 208
(top left) courtesy Sam McElroy; photograph on page 96 (bottom left) courtesy Antonello Venditti; photographs on page 204
(bottom) and page 288 (top left) courtesy I Beni e le Attività Culturali della Campania
Map by Allison Colpoys
Typeset in High Fiber and Adobe Garamond by Post Pre-press Group, Brisbane, Queensland
Colour reproduction by Splitting Image, Clayton, Victoria
Printed in China by 1010 Printing International Limited

National Library of Australia
Cataloguing-in-Publication data:

Tabberer, Amanda.
My Amalfi Coast / Amanda Tabberer.
9781921382314 (pbk.)

Includes index.
Bibliography.

Tabberer, Amanda--Travel--Italy--Amalfi Coast.
Amalfi Coast (Italy)--Description and travel.
Sorrento Peninsula (Italy)--Description and travel.

914.5720493

penguin.com.au